ENERGY CONSERVATION IN BUILDINGS

DR. O.P. JAKHAR

KHANNA BOOK PUBLISHING CO. (P) LTD.

Publisher of Engineering and Computer Books

4C/4344, Ansari Road, Darya Ganj, New Delhi-110002

Phone : 011-23244447-48 **Mobile:** +91-9910909320

E-mail : contact@khannabooks.com

Website : www.khannabooks.com

Dear Readers,

To prevent the piracy, this book is secured with HIGH SECURITY HOLOGRAM on the front title cover. In case you don't find the hologram on the front cover title, please write us to at contact@khannabooks.com or whatsapp us at +91-99109 09320 and avail special gift voucher for yourself.

Specimen of Hologram on front Cover title:

Moreover, there is a SPECIAL DISCOUNT COUPON for you with EVERY HOLOGRAM.

How to avail this SPECIAL DISCOUNT:

Step 1: Scratch the hologram
Step 2: Under the scratch area, your "coupon code" is available
Step 3: Logon to www.khannabooks.com
Step 4: Use your "coupon code" in the shopping cart and get your copy at a special discount
Step 5: Enjoy your reading!

ISBN: 978-93-86173-46-1

ENERGY CONSERVATION IN BUILDINGS by Dr. O.P. Jakhar

Published by:

Khanna Book Publishing Co. (P) Ltd.
Visit us at: **www.khannabooks.com**
Write us at: **contact@khannabooks.com**
CIN: U22110DL1998PTC095547

Printed in India.

PREFACE

This book has the basic motive lo guide the postgraduate and research students working in the field of Energy Conservation. This is to cater the strong need felt by the students pursuing the course on energy Conservation in Buildings during their M. Tech. and PhD. studies. I have tried to compress the subject matter from the view point of research students. The different simulation techniques, such as Power DOE-2, Bsim 2000, e-Quest, which are extensively used in the energy conservation in buildings, have been added for quick references.

The need of energy conservation, history of energy conservation and different passive cooling techniques in building tor hot and dry climate or Rajasthan has been explained in detail. The book has also explored the need and process of energy auditing in building as per the ECBC codes.

A sincere effort has also been made to explain concepts of green building, energy efficient building, radiation cooling in hot and dry climate of Rajasthan and some historical ancient energy efficient buildings of Rajasthan. Readers are requested to communicate the comments, suggestions to improve the book.

Dr. O.P. Jakhar

CONTENTS

1 Introduction

1.1 General Discussion

In India and specially in Rajasthan where atmosphere temperature are very hot and dry for about three fourth part of an year, space, conditioning becomes necessary to ensure good quality of life. Indoor comfort in modern building is generally achieved by consuming large amount of electricity that for its generation usually requires consumption of fossil fuel and causes commission of harmful pollutants like HC, CO, CO_2, NOx, SOx etc.

It is interesting to note that 60% of the total electricity generated in the world is utilized in spaced conditioning. In countries like India, where there is a big gap between energy demand and its supply, use of energy for spaced conditioning will be at the cost energy for other essential or developmental activities. Over past three years, consumption of electricity for space conditioning in India ahs increased at more than 10% per year as compared to about 6.13% growth rate in aggregate demand of electricity. Differences in above figures shows necessity of controlling the growth in electricity consumption for space conditioning to move in tandem with other activities in the country.

Since the demand for better quality of life is increasing continuously day by day, it has become extremely important to find ways for satisfying need of space conditioning with minimum use of scarcely available energy in the country. There are two ways for space conditioning, one is by using active systems and second is through use of passive systems. An active system requires energy, usually in the form of electricity for its operation. Whereas a passive system works in the natural way towards maintaining indoor comfort, using a combination of suitable building materials, proper orientation of buildings, proper layout with respect to neighboring building, using proper shading devices, using natural ventilation, cooling and many other routes. Since building account for large amount of energy consumption in the country, appropriate building designs involving clean and efficient techniques and materials may help to reducing the total energy consumption in the country. It can also help to provide better quality of life to citizens even with shortage of conventional energy.

It has been found that actual performance of the buildings in rural life situations differ from the expected results based on simulation studies. In this work it is planned to conduct experimental validation of simulation results with existing buildings for finding reasons, efforts will be made to refine exiting models for bringing simulation results closer to actual performance. Demand for energy is increasing at on alarming rate and is likely to increase with the increasing pace of industrialization/urbanization. It is reported that oil, natural gas, coal and electricity constitute major source of energy. Further the gap between the production of indigenous crude oil and demand for petroleum product has been increasing by 37%.

1.2 Energy Consumption and Environment

Energy and environment are critical constituents of physical development of the built environment. Hence energy conservation and environmental quality have been widely acknowledged as important parameter of buildings design. It is necessary to understand the strong interaction between architecture and physical development and establisher its importance with environment. Therefore, the energy conscious strategy for buildings emphasizes integration of several environmental factors, inter alia to achieve by desirable ventilation, utilizing day lighting and using appropriate thermal design of buildings for space conditioning. The electricity demand has been changing due to fuel substitution, and increased industrialization and urbanization. The peak demand has gone much above the average demand causing peak shortage of about 18 to 20% as compared to 8 to 10% average shortage in the electricity. The sectoral energy consumption of 499 billion kWh used in year 2007-2009 in shown in Fig. 1.1.

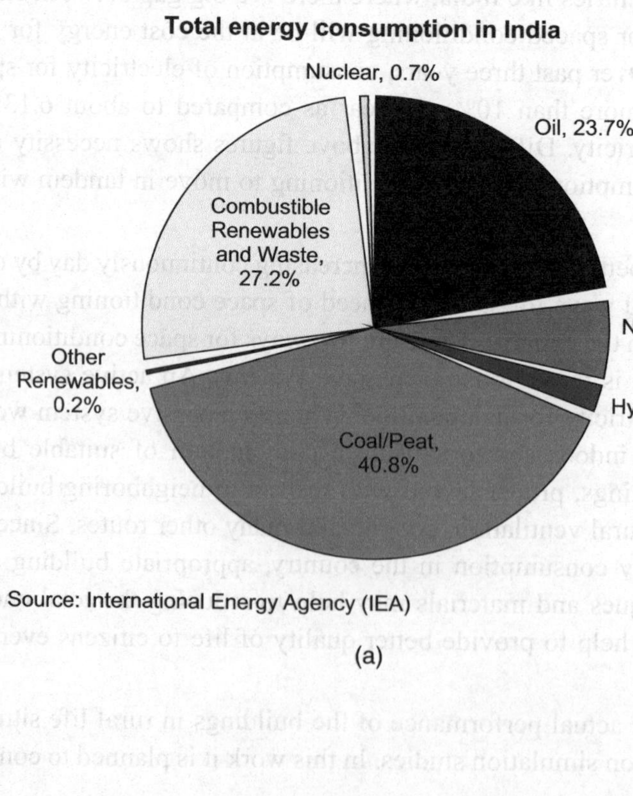

(a)

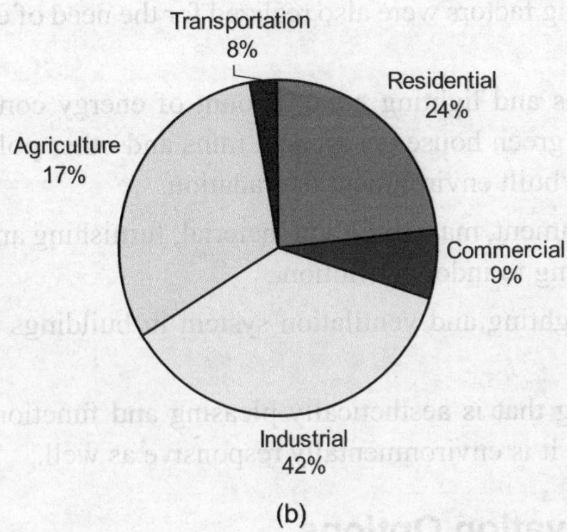

Fig.1.1: Sectoral consumption of electricity in India (Source energy statistics 2017)

In residential and commercial sector there has been a rapid increase in the consumption of power at the rate of about 13.2%. The urbanization trends and increasing comfortable living styles have been the main reasons for growing consumption of electricity. The electricity consumption in residential and commercial buildings is given by figs. 1.2(a) and 1.2(b).

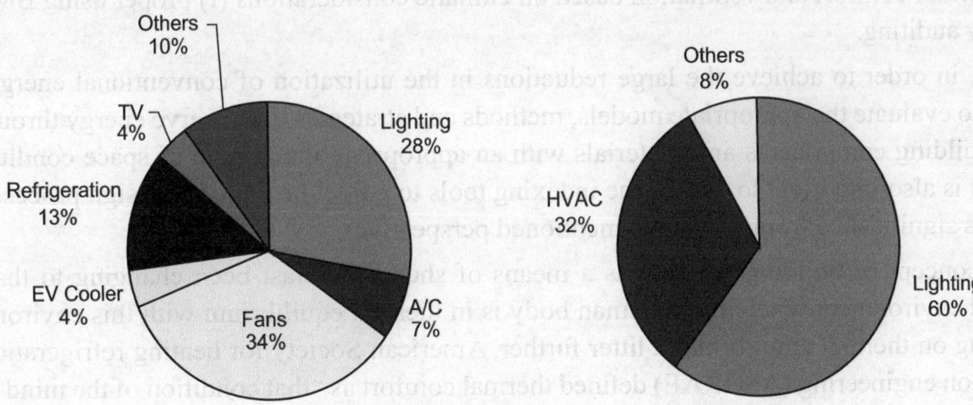

Fig.1.2:

Electricity consumption in buildings is approximately 45% of the total consumption in the country. In western in countries, efforts are being made to bring down the annual energy consumption to the level of 50 kWh/m^2 as Bansal et al (2001). This is possible only through a services of measures comprehensively undertaken in the building design and selection of building materials. The design profession has changed significantly during the last two decades. The reasons attributed include high escalation in energy prices, electricity shortage, along with high concerns over pollution, environmental degradation and resource depletion.

In addition, the following factors were also realized for the need of energy conservation in built environmental.

- Climatic conditions and lighting great amount of energy combustion of fossil, fuels in power plants adds green house gases, acid rains and other pollutants to the environment and also add to the built environment degradation.
- Inside built environment, many building material, furnishing and finishes give off toxic by products contributing to indoor pollution.
- Poorly designed lighting and ventilation system in buildings can induce headaches and fatigue.
- Creating a building that is aesthetically pleasing and functionally active is no longer a good design unless it is environmentally responsive as well.

1.3 Energy Conservation Options

A built environment consumes major share of energy consumption, it is essential to conserve energy in built forms. The literature reveals, that various means to achieve energy conservation in buildings are (a) designing for adequate day lighting, or efficient artificial lighting or controls (b) improving thermal performance for summer and winter (c) reducing heat transfer through windows (d) provision for sufficient ventilation (e) appropriate incursion so as to ensured desired lighting levels, thermal comfort and ventilation based on climatic considerations (f) proper using BMS and (g) energy auditing.

Thus, in order to achieve the large reductions in the utilization of conventional energy, it is essential to evaluate the appropriate models, methods and strategies to conserve energy through the various building components and materials with an appropriate integration of space conditioning options. It is also important to evolve the indexing tools to guide the building design process. This research is significance from the above mentioned perspectives.

The concept of buildings merely as a means of shelter has fast been changing to that of a controlled environment wherein the human body is in thermal equilibrium with this environment. Elucidating on thermal equilibrium a litter further, American Society for heating refrigeration and air condition engineering (ASHRAE) defined thermal comfort as "that condition of the mind which expresses satisfaction with the thermal environment". Although vernacular structures as evident from various literature used indigenous techniques for manipulating the internal environment, today with the advent of technologies, this thermal comfort is achieved by the use of mechanical equipment such as convectors, air conditioners etc. A study of global energy consumption reveals that 45% is used in heating, cooling and lighting of building and further 10% is used in building construction. A study of the building is the United Kingdom shows that for newly designed buildings it is possible to have 50% reduction in energy consumption through energy efficient building design while for exiting buildings a reduction of 25% is possible (Clarke and Mauer, 1991).

A lot of conventional fuel is used to ensure comfortable thermal condition inside residential buildings. This is not only depleting the limited sources available all over the world, but also creating an environmental problem by emitting CO_2 and other polluting gases, which will result in disaster climatic changes.

On the other hand, there are several renewable natural resources, which can be employed to heat or cool a building. For example solar energy in the form of ventilation, can be used to cool a building in summer. Shape of a building its orientation, proper placement of window, providing window with suitable size overhangs, providing proper glazing in windows, all play important role in passive heating and cooling of a building. By providing inertia of the building and that way large variation in the outside environment temperature are effectively attenuated. [Livoni, 1976, Mazria, 1977].

Trees, vegetation and water collection in the vicinity of a building also plays significant role in modulating the inside temperature of a building. These passive cooling techniques have been very successfully used in ancient time all over the world. Oil crisis of 1974 has renewed interest in them.

In this study we have made an attempt to see the effect of shading, ventilation and insulation, on the inside temperature of a building. Details of the study are given in the succeeding chapters. Although these passive cooling techniques have been studied earlier, we have made an attempt to study these in Indian climatic conditions. In case of passive cooling there are definite limit to the degree of cooling that can be achieved. In sever climates where higher atmospheric temperature is processes may prove inadequate for ensuring thermal comfort within the buildings. The requirement of building design for mechanical cooling conflict with those for natural cooling while former require a compact building with less external surface area, amore extended building which can make use of natural ventilation is more appropriate for the latte. Backup mechanical cooling systems for naturally cooled buildings will therefore, be quite inefficient and for this reason it is not common to have back up cooling for such buildings. The case for natural cooling is thus very different from that of solar heating.

A large proportion of the world's population lives in warm and hot climatic zones. It is also in these regions that sufficient economic and energy are not available to employ mechanical cooling in buildings. Many of the natural cooling systems developed in the temperate countries are not usable in the overheated zones, because of dissidences in the socio-cultural patterns. The sub urban single story house type which has been the subject of natural cooling research in USA is not usable in the over populated developing countries because this house type makes insufficient that this particular buildings form is also poorly adopted to minimizing solar heat gain. Thus the used for cooling in such buildings is likely to be much greater than in other types of buildings that may be taller and less exposed to solar radiation.

It is with this back ground that the author has studied the buildings of Bikaner was well as Rajasthan, analyzed their natural cooling design features and measured environmental parameters to establish their effectiveness. To enable some these design features to be used in the changed cultural context of present day, urban areas, the relative solar efficiency of buildings has been studied.

1.4 Simulation Tools

There are various tools for analyzing performance of building in varying climatic conditions. Such tools are Power DOE, e-Quest, Energy Plus, Bism, Ecotect, TRNSYS and few other available. By using these tools buildings can be simulated for load calculation with application of different methods for energy conservation in active space conditioning devices under any set of climatic conditions. Such tools are useful for designing and doing cost benefit analysis for various energy conservation options in a purposed building.

The heat flow paths can be considered to be equivalent to an electrical network of time dependent resistance and capacitances subjected to time dependent potential differences (Gupta and Raychandhary, 1963). In such an analogy, the resultant electrical currents in each branch of network are equivalent to the heat flows encountered within the between the building elements. To represent this transfer equations are required. These equations are highly interrelated and therefore should be solved simultaneously. This tedious task of converting the building heat flow paths into mathematical from and solving the equations thus formed for getting an outputs is done by what is called simulation tools. The simulation tools can predict the formal functional, economic and technical characteristics of building performance (Cross, 1986). Although it is possible to assess the thermal performance of a proposed building by various methods, such as full scale filed experiments, laboratory test etc., but these are cost and labour intensive methods can deal with any level of complexity. There is no restriction in the input parameters and any numbers of parametric variation can be taken into account. Broadly speaking a simulation model can be used to answer such questions as (Clarke and Maver 1991).

- What is the maximum demand for heating cooling and illumination and where and when do they occur? What are causal factors?
- What will be the effect of a particular design strategy, such as adopting "super insulation" specialist glazing system or using passive techniques?
- What is the effect of building performance with orientation option?
- How will the building perform thermally if the choice of building materials is changed?
- What is the contribution of a particular passive solar feature to energy saying and comfort level? And so on.

In an effort to address the complexity of these queries and to provide an effective design support, the building simulation tools have received growing attention in the recent years. The simulation tool allows a designer to understand the interrelation between design and performance parameters, identify the potential problem areas, and implement and test appropriate modification to the design. The resultant design is energy conscious with a higher possibility of attaining acceptable comfort levels. For example a building located in a cold climate zone where heating is the predominant requirement simulation can give the output result in the form of the amount of glazing area sufficient for either totally doing away with conventional heating or for efficiently reducing the use of conventional energy.

These building energy analysis models fill a broad range of requirements, from energy audit to the design of new buildings calculations of energy consumptions, policy studies, and theoretical investigations of new retrofit and application of innovative building materials along with the building performance.

The simulation models use different methods for heating and cooling load calculation (Tromeala and Rahola, 1995). In the heat balance or thermal balance method, the load can be calculated by solving the transient heat balance equations for each thermal mode simultaneously. In the weighing factor method, effect of various load component (e.g. solar gains, internal heat gain etc.) are summed up using weighing factors. The weighing factor is calculated separately for each load component and building type using a programme based on the heat balance method (Kalema, 1992). Some of them are based on the weighing factor method like Power DOE 2.1, Energy Plus and e-Quest. After choice of a method the thrust is on the calculation of the transient heat flux through the building elements such as walls, roof etc. These calculations are normally performed by using analytical method's approximate methods and correlation methods (Sodha, 1986). The analytical methods are based on the solution of the governing heat conduction equations appropriate boundary condition.

The correlation methods namely the solar load ratio method developed by Balcomb (1982) and load collector ratio (Bulcomb and McForland 1978) are well known and make use of tabulated values or curves that are location specific. These curves are drived from hourly simulation using large simulation models.

Approximate methods are used extensively for heat load calculations. These include the degree day and steady state methods. Degree days method deals with the seasonal heat losses. This is based on the assumption that an unheated buildings on an average maintains an indoor temperature higher than the outdoor temperature as a higher than the outdoor temperature as a result of casual heat gains. On a day to day basis when the mean daily temperature is 1^0C below the base temperature this difference of 1°C can be used in the heat loss and energy consumption calculations and such a day gives '1' degree. A day with 2°C drop below the base case, or two days with 1^0C drop will give 2 degree days so on (Morkus and Morris, 1980).

1.5 Climatic zones of India

India possesses a variety of climates, ranging from extremely hot desert regions to high altitude locations with severely cold conditions, similar to northern Europe. On the basis of monthly mean data recorded in 233 stations, located in all parts of India, it was found convenient to divide the country into following six climatic zones (Bansal and Minke, 1986):

i. Hot and dry (HD)
ii. Warm and humid (WH)
iii. Moderate (MO)
iv. Cold and cloudy (CC)
v. Cold and sunny (CS)
vi. Composite (CO)

The main determining factor for the classification of the climatic zones, namely air temperature and relative humidity, are those the predominantly influence heat exchange between the human body and the surroundings. The two other factors, namely solar radiation and precipitation, are those that influence building design. Since the data available from the meteorological station does not include absolute values of radiation, it was possible to express this factor in "number of days".

The criteria for the allocation of a station to one of the first five climatic zones is that the defined conditions prevail for more than 6 months. In cases, where none of these categories can be identified for six months or longer, the climatic zone is called "Composite". On this basis, the evaluation of the mean monthly climatic data from the 233 stations led to the delineation of the six climatic zones on the map of India (Figure 1.3).

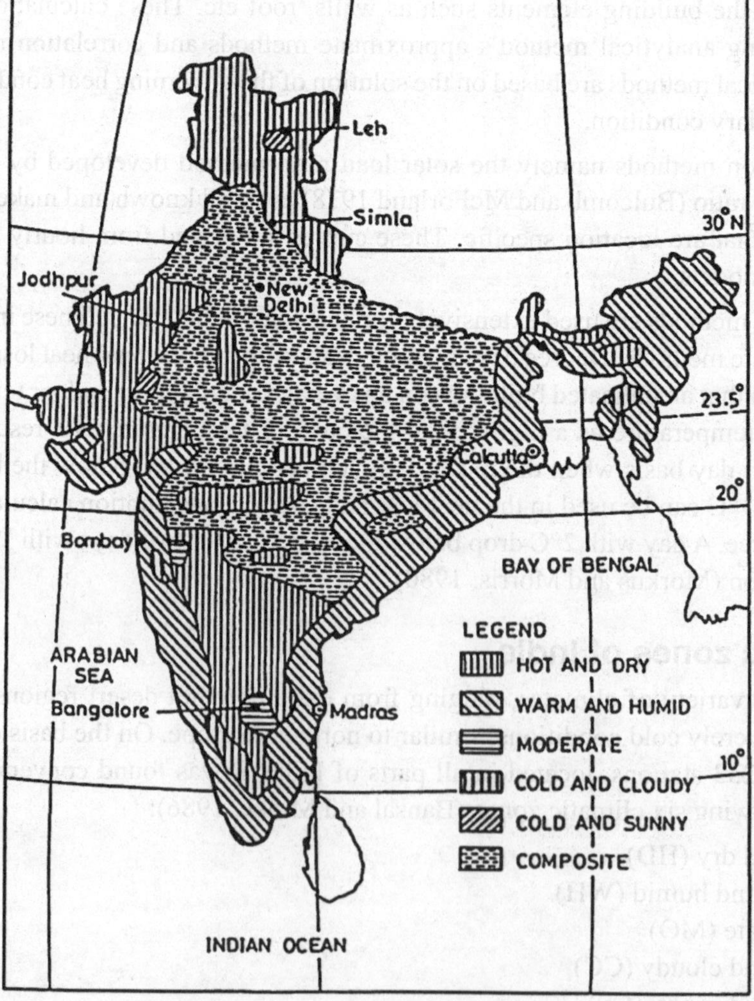

Fig.1.3: Climatic Zones of India

Figure 1.4 shows six locations which can be considered typical of each climatic zone: in Jodhpur 7 months can be classified as hot and dry, in Bombay 10 months are typically warm and humid and Bangalore has moderate conditions also for 10 months of the year. Simla can be called cold and cloudy for 8 months, while Leh is cold and sunny all through the year. Since New Delhi's climate does not correspond of the previous categories for more than half a year, it falls into the composite zone.

Table 1.1: Criteria for the classification of climates

Climatic Zone	Mean Monthly Temperature (°C)	Relative Humidity (%)	Precipitation (mm)	No. of clear days
Hot and dry (HD)	>30	<55	<5	>20
Warm and humid (WH)	>30	>55	>5	<20
Moderate (MO)	25-30	<75	<5	<20
Cold and cloudy (CC)	<25	>55	>5	<20
Cold and sunny (CS)	<25	<55	<5	>20
Composite (CO)	This applies when six months or more do not fall within any of the above categories			

Great amount of energy is consumed in the building sector in the world. World over, distribution of energy consumption in the building sector present a very starling fact that major share of the energy is consumed in the residential sector. The following chart depicts the distribution.

The buildings, due to their design features, have diverse energy consumption standards. The fact that "the newer the building, the lesser the energy consumption" is very obvious from the following:

The above chart tells a story as to how technological and architectural developments have succeeded in reducing energy consumption in the building sector. The world is busy designing and implementing "Near Net Zero Energy Buildings". But this effort has very little for old buildings. Old buildings present a challenge to the world to improve on its energy performance index. With increasing urbanization and globalization, energy consumption in building sector has been on the rise consistently however rise has been very steep in the recent year. India is no different from the world in this regard and following chart depicts that the rate of increase in energy consumption and has been rising every since at a very brisk rate.

Building are responsible for more than half of harmful green house gas emissions in most cities such as New York and London that number can such to more than 70%. The popularity of green buildings as ecofriendly with their own water harvesting and solar power systems is catching in India and the high price is not deterrent. Green buildings also have their own cycling system more than 50% of the building's is covered with glass making it reflect away the sun's rays and helping to keep the inside cool and save the electricity among other eco-friendly measures. Green buildings thus are being headed toward protection of nature and built environment and do socially responsible development. The quality and values inherent to the traditional human response to the environment might be preserved without loss of the advances of science. Science can be applied to various aspects of work, while it is at the same time subordinated to philosophy, faith and spirituality.

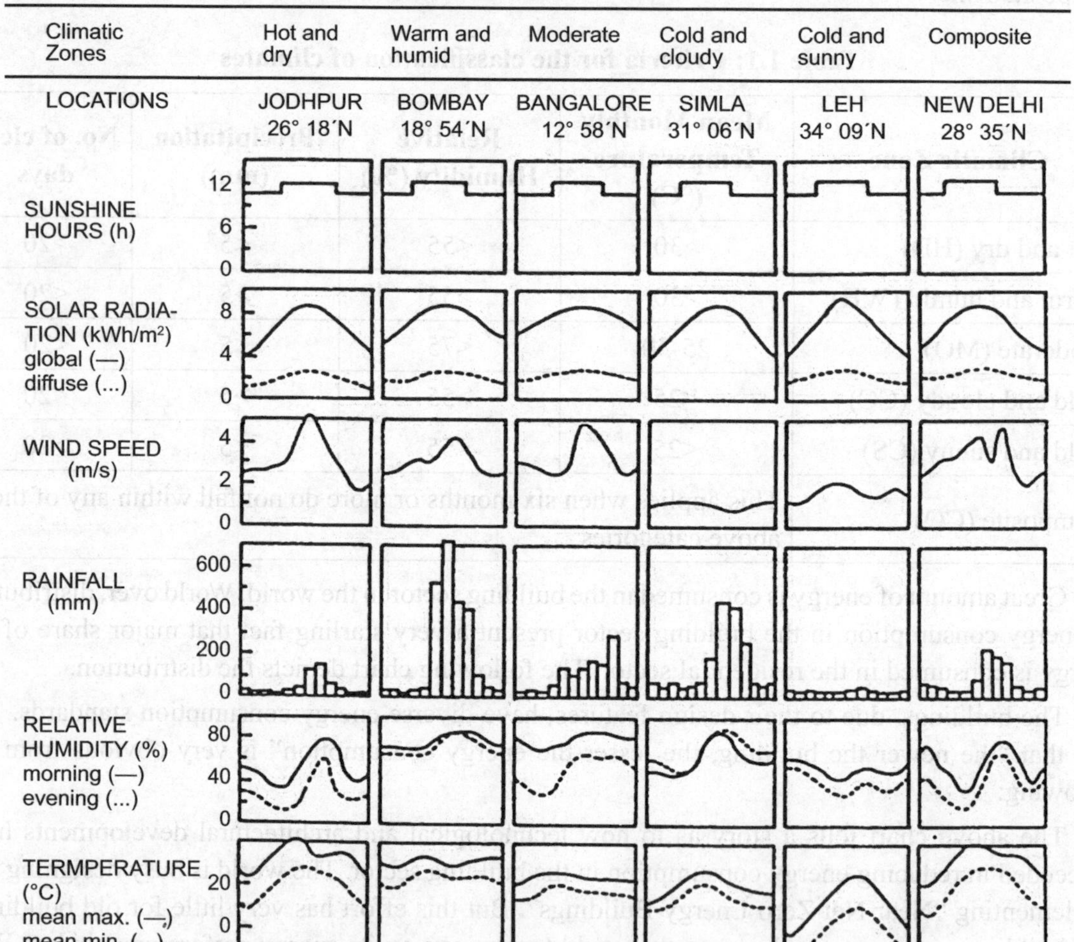

Fig.1.4: Climatic Data Representation of Hot & Dry, Cold & Sunny and Composite Climatic Conditions

The design, construction and maintenance of building have a tremendous impact on our environment and our natural resources. Today there are more than 76 million residential buildings and nearly 5 million commercial buildings in USA. These building together use one-third of all the energy consumed in SUA and two-third of all electricity. By the year 2010, another 38 million buildings are expected to be constructed. The challenge will be to build them smart, so they use a minimum non renewable energy, produce minimum of pollution and cost of energy will be minimum, while increasing the comfort health and safely of the people who live and work in it.

Further buildings are major source of the pollution that causes urban air quality problems and the pollutants that contribute to the climate change. They account for 49% of SO_2 emission, 25% NOx emission and 10% of particulates emissions, all of which damage urban air quality. Building produce 35% of CO_2 emissions which is chief pollutant blamed for climate change. Traditionally building practices often overlook the inter relationships between a building, its components, its surroundings and its occupants. "Typical" building consume more of our resources than necessary, negatively impact the environment and generate a large amount of work. According to Laurence Doxsey former coordinator of the city of Austin Greene builder programme "a standard wood-framed home consumes over one acre of forest and work created during construction averages from 3 to 7 tons". Often, these buildings are costly to operate in terms of conservation would be enormous. Increased private investment in biodiversity business would have the greatest impact in developing nations, where the conservation funding gap is most extreme and where many critically endangered species and habitats are virtually unprotected today.

1.6 Solar Energy

Energy is an essential ingredient in meeting basic human needs for supporting desired standard of living and helping economic growth of the country. The rising global demand for energy has been met to an increasing extent by the use of fossil fuels. However, there has been a realisation that these energy resources are scarce and should be viewed as depleting assets and a sources of green house gases emission. If the countries around the world do not reduce GHG emissions by end of next century, then.

- The temperature of earth will increase by 1 to 3.5°C depending upon population and economic growth.
- Sea level will rise 15 to 90 cm higher than now threatening 92 million people each year with floods.
- Mortality and illness rate will rise, as intensity/'duration of heat waves will increase.
- Rainfall will decrease leading to reduction in food production.

In this context, solar energy has great potential. The solar energy sources hold out a major promise in the direction of meeting out essential energy requirements in the field of domestic, agriculture, transport and industries. These sources are available in abundance in nature and these are economical as well as environmentally sound in the context of India.

1.6.1 World potentials

Total area under the desert in the world about 50×10^6 km^2, of which 20×10^6 km2, receives an average insolation of 583.3 W/m^2 and other 30×10^6 km^2, area receives 291.6 W/m^2. If on an average 8 hours of sunshine per day than solar energy received is 162.2×11^{12} kWh/day, thus 60×10^{15} kWh/year. If only 1% is utilized than it works out to 60×10^{13} kWh/year.

Present energy consumption is 50×10^{12} kWh/year on world basis, hence 10 times more what the world requires.

1.6.2 India's potentials

Total land area 3.28×10^{12} sq. Meter on an average 0.5 kW/m^2 per day solar energy is falling on the land for 300 days in a year. If 1% of this energy only at 105 overall efficiency, than approximate 492×108 kWh/year electricity can be generated.

1.6.3 Solar Passive Architecture

In buildings without mechanical cooling or heating, so long as the outdoor weather conditions are stable, the daily heat flux entering the building equals the heat flux going out. In such conditions, the period during which the building heats up is roughly equal to the period during which the building cools down (fig. 1.5). If it is desired that the average indoor air temperature be lower than average outdoor air temperature, it can be seen from fig. 1.6 that the potential period for natural cooling is reduced while the period for heating is increased. Conversely, if the indoor average temperature is to be higher than the average outdoor temperature (fig. 1.7), the period for heating is reduced while the cooling period is increased. This is independent of the phase lag due to the mass of the structure. Since the heat flux going out must still equal the heat flux coming in, it follows that the rate at which heat flows in through the building fabric cannot be the same as the rate at which heat flows out. Because the heat flow in and out of a building element depends upon its thermal transmittance, a variable heat flow can be ensured only by a building fabric of which the thermal transmittance properties can be changed at wall. For hot climates this means a high resistance to incoming heat and a low resistance for outgoing heat. Buildings loss and gain heat by radiation, convection, conduction and evaporation. Each of these four modes of heat transfer can be used for altering thermal transmittance.

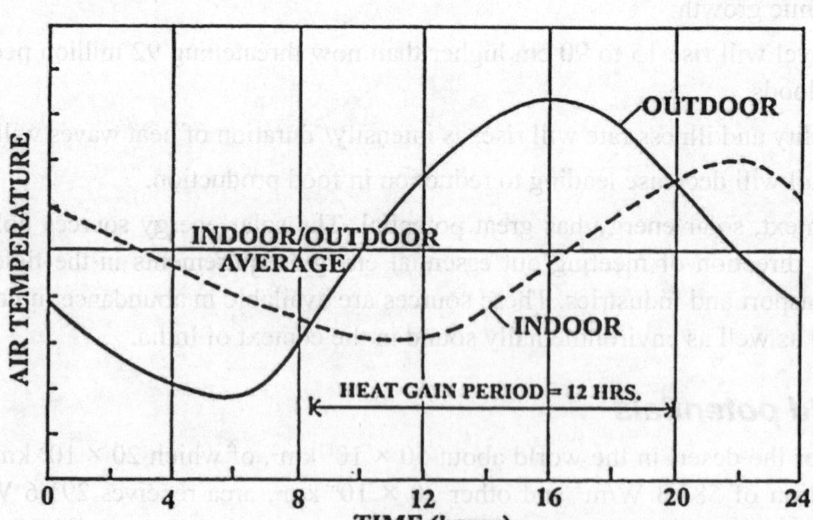

Fig.1.5: The average internal temperature equals average external temperature

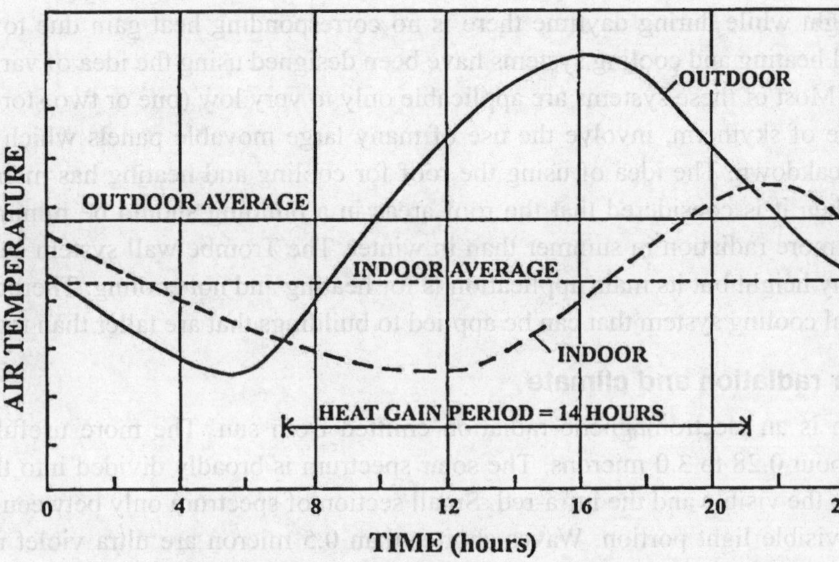

Fig.1.6: The average internal temperature less average external temperature

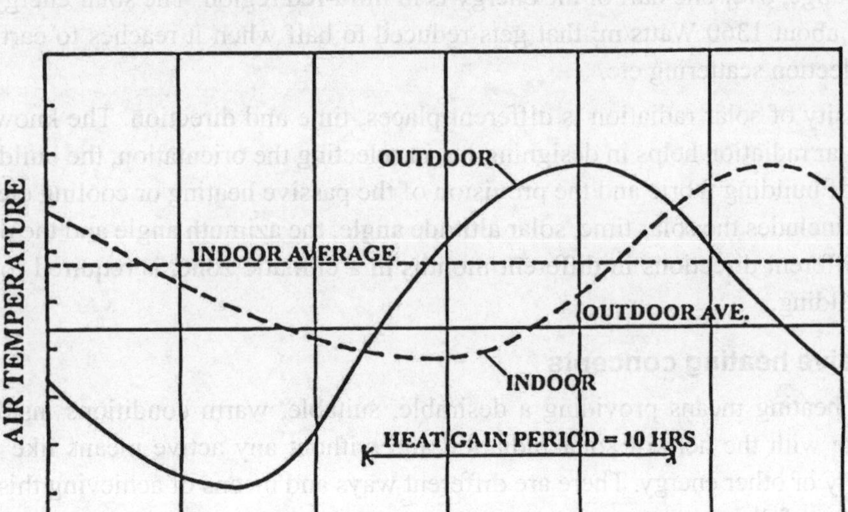

Fig.1.7: The average internal temperature greater average external temperature

In solar heated buildings, the use of glass permits short wave radiation to enter the building but does not allow long wave radiation to go out. Thus solar heated buildings can maintain indoors an average temperature higher than outdoors. Movable insulation is sometimes used along with glass, which also alters the heat flow by conduction. In naturally cooled buildings, selective ventilation i.e. ventilation only during the cool night hours, causes rapid convective heat loss while convective heat gain is much lower. Night time roof surface evaporation of such buildings also cause rapid heat loss at night while during daytime there is no corresponding heat gain due to evaporation. Several natural heating and cooling systems have been designed using the idea of variable thermal transmittance. Most of these systems are applicable only to very low (one or two storey) buildings and in the case of skytherm, involve the use of many large movable panels which are prone to mechanical breakdown. The idea of using the roof for cooling and heating has many limitations particularly when it is considered that the roof areas in a building should be minimized as they intercept a lot more radiation in summer than in winter. The Trombe wall system can be used on buildings of any height but its main application is for heating and not cooling. Therefore, the need to find a natural cooling system that can be applied to buildings that are taller than two storeys.

1.6.3.1 Solar radiation and climate

Solar radiation is an electromagnetic radiation emitted from sun. The more useful wavelength ranges from about 0.28 to 3.0 microns. The solar spectrum is broadly divided into three regions: the ultra violet, the visible and the infra-red. Small section of spectrum only between 0.4 and 0.76 micron is the visible light portion. Waves shorter than 0.5 micron are ultra violet radiation and longer than 0.76 microns are known as infrared. Although the peak intensity of solar radiation is in the visible range, over one half of the energy is in infra-red region. The solar energy at the outer atmosphere is about 1360 Watts/m^2 that gets reduced to half when it reaches to earth because of absorption reflection scattering etc.

The intensity of solar radiation is different places, time and direction. The knowledge of the intensity of solar radiation helps in designing i.e. in selecting the orientation, the building material, the thickness of building fabric and the provision of the passive heating or cooling elements. Solar geometry that includes the solar time, solar altitude angle, the azimuth angle and the data of hourly variation in different directions in different months in a climatic zone, is required for the passive design of a building.

1.6.3.2 Passive heating concepts

Solar passive heating means providing a desirable, suitable, warm conditions inside a building in cold climate with the help of solar radiation and without any active means like an appliance using electricity or other energy. There are different ways and means of achieving this aim of solar passive heating as follows:

1.6.3.3 Direct gain

It is a simple method in which sunlight is directly admitted into the building through a window or the glass wall. Sun rises in east and set in west but it always moves southward. The altitude of the sun is high in summer and low in winters so it can come inside a building for more time in winter from a window facing south. In summers as it moves on a higher level so a sunshade can easily prevent it. Thus the south direction is the most useful one with respect to the solar passive architecture. In this simple method a window having a single glass panel allows the short wave solar radiation inside the room and as it heats up the simple method a window having a single glass panel allows the short wave solar radiation inside the room and as it heats up the belongings of the rooms they emit the long wave radiation. Glass is opaque to the long wave radiation and thus does not allow the heat to escape. But as the outside cols air is in contact with the glass and reduces its temperature by convection, we provide two layers of the glass. This is known as the double glazed window. The air cavity in between the two layers of the glass also improves its heat insulation capacity. And the overall heat loss coefficient is reduced. Night insulation is also used that can be rolled over the window glass so the heat loss in the nights can be minimized. Knowing the 'g' value that is the solar gain factor and the overall heat loss coefficient the optimum size of the windows can be calculated.

(a) (b)

Fig.1.8: Natural lighting and ventilation building

1.6.3.4 Indirect methods

In these methods the heat of solar radiation is stored in some medium and then transferred to the room. Actually the heat gain inside the room is oscillating because of the hourly variation of solar radiation. A more effective method for reducing the swings in the room temperature is to introduce a thermal storage wall between the solar radiation and the living space (room). In these methods a wall is constructed in the south direction that receives the solar energy throughout the day and gets heated up. The solar heat gets transferred to the inner side of the wall in due course of time and then by radiation and convection gets inside the room for space heating. The solar energy is introduced into the room in an indirect way as a result of convection and long wave radiation emitted by the thermal wall that gets heated due to the absorbed energy at its surface. To make this process more effective following methods are there in use:

1.6.3.5 Trombe wall

Trombe wall is a massive wall of masonry or concrete constructed in south direction and blackened on the outer surface. The outer most layer of this arrangement is a double layer glass wall. As explained earlier the short wave solar radiation comes through glass, the black surface of the wall absorbs it much efficiently and gets heated up. The sun's rays also heat up the air between the glass wall and the solid wall. There are two vents at the top and bottom of the solid wall as shown in the diagram below. The heated air becomes lighter and lifts up and enters the room through the upper vent. The cold heavy air from the room is dragged to take the empty space of this air and thus a cycle starts and the rooms get heated up. The heat input into the room can be adjusted by controlling the flow of air through dampers. In the night time these vents may be closed. The heat absorbed by the blackened thick wall gets transferred in some hours (say 10 hours) due to the time lag property and reaches to the inner side of the wall in the night time. From there it gets transferred to the room by the long wave radiation emitted from the wall.

The double-glazing of wall reduces the heat loss from it air cavity between the two glass surfaces also works as an insulation as air is the bad conductor of heat. However a rolling sheet may cover the whole wall in the nights to have night insulation.

Trombe wall is essentially a thick wall facing south, with the outer surface blackened and glazed. The storage mass may be concrete, adobe, stone or bricks, vents provided both at the upper and lower ends facilitate air circulation from the space between the glazing and wall to the interior of the room (Fig. 1.3). The glazing of the south black wall intercepts the solar radiation during the day, heating the air in the duct formed by the glazing and the wall. The hot air rises up and enters the building through the upper vent drawing in the cool air from the room through the lower vents. The heat input into the room can be controlled by adjusting the flow of air through the dampers. Closing the vents during the night time creates a dead space in the duct, reducing the convective heat losses from the outer surface of the hot wall to the ambient air. Covering the glazing during off-sunshine hours further helps in reducing heat losses to the ambient. in addition to conduction heat through the wall, the heat flux entering the living space due to the air circulation, can be estimated from the following analysis:

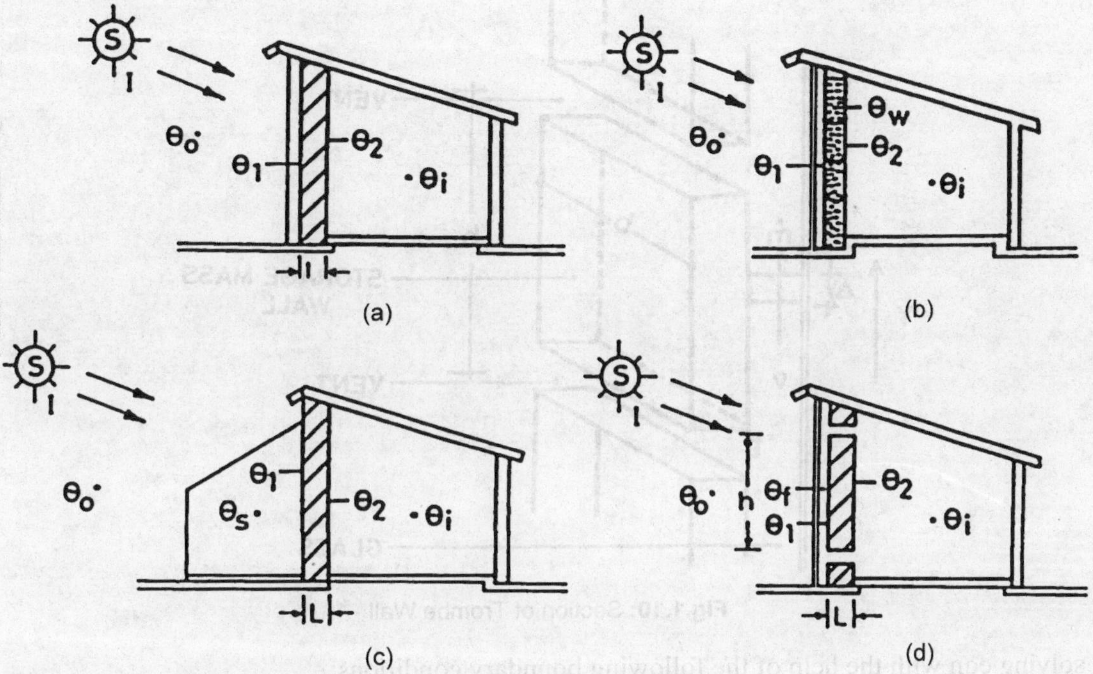

Fig.1.9: Configuration of the passive heating concept (a) mass wall (b) water wall (c) solarium and (d) trombe wall

The total energy input to the room is the sum of the energy conducted through the wall and convected into the room through the upper vent. The energy balance at the absorbing surface (x=0) and the inside surface (x=L) of the Trombe wall can be written as:

$$q = h_{og}(\theta_i - \theta_o) - \alpha_s I$$

$$q = \frac{k(\theta_2 - \theta_1)}{L} + m\,C_{pa}(\theta_{os} - \theta_i)$$

$$\frac{k(\theta_2 - \theta_1)}{L} = h_i(\theta_i - \theta_2)$$

The temperature rise of an elementary area ($b\Delta y$) of Trombe wall be (fig. 1.8) can be written as,

$$mCpa\,\frac{\partial \theta_f}{\partial f}\,\Delta y = h_f(\theta_1 - \theta_f)\,b\,\Delta y$$

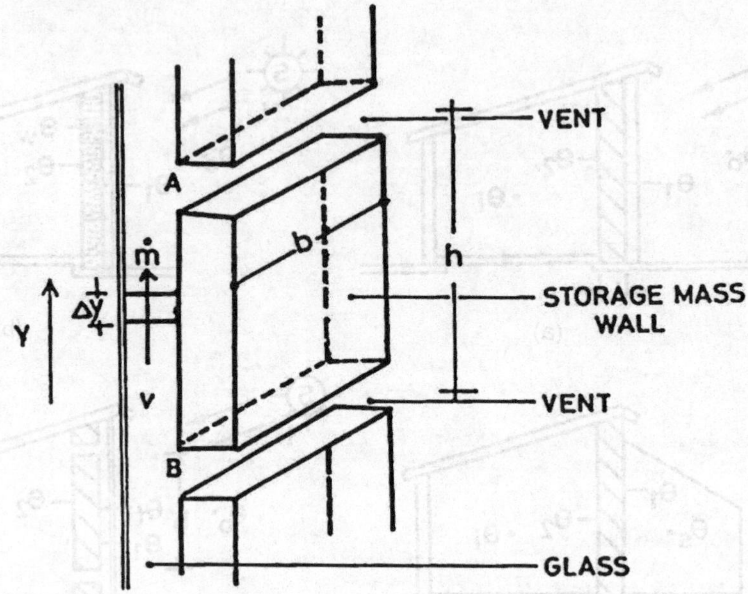

Fig.1.10: Section of Trombe Wall

On solving eqn with the help of the following boundary conditions;

at $y = 0, \theta_f = \theta_i$

and at $y = h, \theta_f = \theta_{os}$

the final expression derived is an given below:

$$\theta_{os} = \theta_i \exp(-\beta h) + \theta_1 [1 - \exp(-\beta h)]$$

where

$$\beta = \frac{h_f b}{MC_{pa}}$$

therefore

$$\frac{\rho_1 - \rho_2}{\rho_2} = \frac{\Delta\rho}{\rho_2} = \frac{T_2 - T_1}{T_1} = \frac{\Delta T}{T_1} = \frac{\Delta\theta}{\theta_i + 273}$$

or

$$v = \sqrt{\frac{2\Delta\theta\, g_a\, h}{\theta_i + 273}}$$

where $\Delta q = \theta_{os} - \theta_i$

The above expression for v has been derived on the basis that there are no frictional or other losses in the flow. In a real situation, however, the buoyancy velocity is smaller than that given by eqn and a dimensionless Froude number $F_r \leq 1$ has therefore to be added; to get the expression as given below:

$$v = F_r \sqrt{\frac{2 \Delta\theta \, g_a \, h}{\theta_i + 273}}$$

The value of F_r – 0.5 has been taken for calculations.

The mass flow rate (m) is thus given by

$$m = rA_a v$$

The heat flux into the room (q) is found by iteratively calculating θ_1 and substituting this value of θ_1 in eqn.

1.6.3.6 Water Wall

Water wall is based on the same principle as the mass wall except that water is used as the storage material. The masonry wall in the mass wall concept is replaced by drums full of water staked over each other. The exterior face of the drums is usually painted black or a dark color for maximum absorption of solar radiation. The drums can be replaced by containers such as tin cans, bottles, tubes, bins, barrels, bags and complete water walls. Water wall transfers heat through the wall by convection.

At steady state,

$$\begin{aligned} q &= h_{og} (\theta_1 - \theta_i) - \alpha_s I \\ &= h_{wl} (\theta_w - \theta_1) \\ &= h_{w2} (\theta_2 - \theta_w) \\ &= h_i (\theta_i - \theta_2) \end{aligned}$$

Adding and rearranging eqns, the heat flux can be given by eqn, with Uw value given by,

$$U_w = \left[\frac{1}{h_g} + \frac{1}{h_{wl}} + \frac{1}{h_{w2}} + \frac{1}{h_i} \right]^{-1}$$

1.6.3.7 Solarium

Solarium is a passive heating concept that integrates the direct gain approach with the thermal storage of passive system (Balcomb, 1978). It consists of a sunspace situated at the south end of the house and is separated from the main house by a thick storage wall. This integrated system greatly reduces the temperature swings in the living space of the main house. The solarium provides a comfortable environment for sunbath and other activities in the sun un winter.

The glass enclosure (sunspace) receives heat by direct gain while the living space receives heat by indirect gain, through the storage wall.

At steady state,

$$q = h_{ws}(\theta_1 - \theta_s) - \alpha_s I$$

$$= \frac{k(\theta_2 - \theta_1)}{L}$$

$$= h_i(\theta_i - \theta_2)$$

Also, the heat loss through the glass is equal to the heat loss at the wall,

$$Aw\, h_{ws}(\theta_s - \theta_1) = A_G h_{GO}(\theta_o - \theta_s)$$

Solving and rearranging eqns the heat flux (q) is given by eqn with U_w value given by,

$$U_w = \left[\frac{1}{h_{eff}} + \sum_n \frac{L_n}{k_n} + \frac{1}{h_i}\right]^{-1}$$

Where,

$$heff = \frac{A_G h_O h_W}{A_G h_O + A_W h_w}$$

1.6.3.8 Sun space (attached solarium)

This method is a combination of direct and indirect gains. The living space is provided with a thermal storage wall on the south side. One glass space is attached to this south wall. The glass enclosure called as the sunspace receives heat by direct gain. This heat is absorbed by the wall and then transmitted to the room in due course of time (time lag) depending upon the coefficient of thermal conductivity of the wall material and the thickness of the wall. The sunspace may be used for recreating or for growing plants etc.

1.6.3.9 Solar passive cooling

As discussed earlier the solar air conditioning and refrigeration are different techniques in which the solar energy is utilizes to evaporate some refrigerant and the cold so obtained is used for cooling the building or the refrigerator. In the passive cooling the buildings are constructed in such a way that the sun may not heat them up so vigorously. The walls are designed with a desirable orientation (longer axis pointing towards east and west). By adopting these techniques the peak cooling power demand of a building can be reduced. These techniques are ventilation, evaporation, infrared transfer to the sky, and the earth contact cooling etc.

One way is to reduce the unnecessary thermal load on the buildings. This includes the direct exposure of useful living space to the harsh sunrays. The internal heating load by electrical light can be replaced by diffused day lighting as far as possible. In general the thermal load can be minimized by the following ways:

1.6.3.10 Reduction of direct beam radiation by shading

The main source of heating of a building is the direct solar radiation falling on a building. In hot and dry climatic conditions the building should be constructed so that they may have either a mutual shading, or the sunshades, horizontal and inclined louvers, movable screens or trees (particularly on west side) and plants. The sunshades should be designed in such a way, as shown below that the summer sun (high altitude) may not enter inside the building while the winter sun (lower altitude) may not be obstructed.

1.6.3.11 Reduction of conduction of heat through walls and roof

The outer surface of walls and roof get heated due to the direct sunrays or the ambient air. The direct sunrays on the roof or walls increase the temperature much above the temperature of the ambient air due to the absorption of the solar radiation. This temperature is known as the solar temperature. For example if the air temperature is 45^{0}C the solair temperature surface temperature may be as high as 65^{0}C depending upon the absorptivity and the intensity of solar radiation. This high surface temperature gets transferred through the walls and roof and depending upon their thickness and coefficient of thermal conductivity of wall material, takes time to travel and reach inside the room. As the intensity and time duration for which the solar radiation falls on a particular direction wall is different the heat gain through them is also different. But as, it is maximum on a horizontal surface so heat gain through the roof is maximum. This is evident from the following table for a particular place for example.

The expected share of heat gain from different components of building

	Roof (%)	North (%)	South (%)	East (%)	West (%)
Summer	48-51	6-13	0-2	19-20	19-20
Winter	28-34	0	35-44	14-15	14-15

This shows the importance of orientation and the protection of roof. If the longer axis of the building points towards the east and west then the longer faces are towards south and north. The south direction gets maximum heat transferred in winter and minimum in summer so beneficial in both climates. But the main thing is the roof. The roofing should have a light colour to absorb least heat. The roof should have an insulating property so that the lesser heat is transferred. For this sometimes, inverted earthen pots are kept on the roof to increase its thickness and entrap the air that increases the insulting power.

The most advantageous and powerful method is evaporative cooling of the roof. It a thin layer of water can be spread and maintained on the roof, this water shall evaporate. Some latent heat is required for evaporation and this heat shall be taken from the surface of roof that is in contact of the water. This shall drastically reduce the temperature of the roof and this effect shall go upto the inside of the room. C.B.R.I Roorkee has done great research in this field and found it very much suitable, feasible and economical solution. This can be used even in the multi-storey buildings. The availability of water is of course a limitation. It is suggested here to use non-foul wastewater (kitchen and bathroom water) for this purpose. The texturing of outer surface may help to some extent. The uneven surfaces developed by texturing, provides some shade to the wall surface and this also helps in reducing the absorption of the solar heat.

Use of light paints on wall is also beneficial as it reduces the absorption of solar radiation.

1.6.3.12 Special method of passive cooling like wind towers

A wind tower is a tall construction that absorbs the solar heat during the day and releases it to the cool air at night. The next day the walls are cool. When there is no wind hot ambient air enters the tower through the openings in the sides and is cooled when it comes in contact with the tower. Since the cooler air is denser it sinks down through the tower creating a downdraught. Doors in the lower part of the tower open into the central portion of the building. When there is no wind at night the tower operates like a chimney. Heat that has been stored in the walls during the day warms the cool night air in the tower and goes up, as it is lighter. Thus the cycle gets completed and the tower keeps on working next day. The only problem is the massive construction of the wind tower.

1.6.3.13 Passive heating and cooling

The temperature of the ground below a few meters of the surface is always throughout the year. This is the reason that we get cold water in summers and hot waters from a tube well (underground water). This concept is used in the earth air tunnels to heat or cool a buildings.

The constant temperature below the earth is dependent on the surface conditions, that is, shaded, dry or wet. As the surface temperatures of the exposed surfaces are much more (solar temperature) so the underground temperatures are also more. The following table shows the approximate expected temperature below a depth of 4 m from the surface for different ground conditions.

Table 1.2: Temperature below earth surface

Surface condition	Ground temperature
Dry, exposed to sun	27.5°C
Dry, shaded	18.5°C
Wet, exposed to sun	21.5°C
Wet shaded	21.0°C

In this system a tunnel is made below the earth at some convenient position. A small fan is installed on one side of it to pump the air into the tunnel. The forced air at the constant temperatures as shown in the table 1.2, is circulated in the building by different ducts. This provides a comfortable temperature (hot in winters and cold in summers) throughout the year. One such earth air tunnel is working in the 'mud house' constructed in an Indo-German Project in I.I.T. Delhi.

These are some the elements of solar passive architecture. There are many other features like the roof pond sky therm, very therm wall, earth bermed structures, combination of sensitive and evaporative cooling, courtyard effect etc.

(a) (b)

Fig.1.11: Natural lighting and ventilation building

2 History of Energy Conservation in Buildings

The internal thermal environment of any building is effected from the response of the building changing external climatic fluctuations which repeat themselves in daily cycle (which as a period of 24 hrs) and in the annual cycle (period 365 days), depending upon the geographical location of the site. Near the poles, the annual cycle is of maximum importance while at the equator the daily cycle plays a major role for a determining the quality of shelter needed. The main climatic parameters that influence the thermal load at any location are:

i. Solar radiation (its intensity, direction and duration of sunshine hours)

ii. Ambient air temperature

iii. Humidity and precipitation

iv. Wind speed and direction

v. Clearness of the sky

Solar radiation in three forms affects the performance of any building, namely, direct, diffused and reflected radiation. For achieving the required internal environment, an attempt should be made to design the building taking into account the diurnal movement of the sun for maximum natural light and minimum heat load.

The first step to achieve natural cooling or for controlling energy consumption for cooling ion a building is through reduction of thermal load.

Thermal load can be classified into two main categories:

i. Exterior load due to climate

ii. Internal load due to appliances, cooking, bathing etc.

Further, there are three main causes of exterior load:

a. Penetration of direction beam sunlight

b. Transfer of heat through walls, roof etc.

c. Infiltration of outside air.

Many examples of ancient architecture have special design feature that provide comfortable living conditions without use conventional from of energy. The shape and orientation of buildings, the arrangement of openings, use of shading devices, landscaping, creation of heat sinks and numerous other features offer opportunity for taking maximum advantage of climate for natural space conditioning.

The thermal response of a building may be determined from the heart gain factors through various structural element viz. walls, window, roof and floor, the internal heat loads, rate of ventilation, occupancy schedules and trends etc. The transfer of heat between a building and its environment largely depend upon the overall conductance of structure, the degree of exposure to weather including sunshine and existing temperature differences between inside and outside. Other parameters like wind velocity also effect this value. All of these features can be modeled using heat transfer equations.

In recent years, various mathematical techniques have been developed for modeling heat gain and thermal load in buildings. Various models developed so far be divided into three basic categories:

i. Approximate methods
ii. Correlation methods
iii. Analytical methods

Modeling of heat transfer and cooling load requirement is necessary for any building keeping in mind the objective of minimizing energy consumption for controlling internal environment. Such modeling covers analysis of effect of external environmental features such as solar radiation, wind, natural light, moisture and internal sources of thermal load such as lighting, electrical appliances, occupancy etc.

Use of natural cooling techniques can reduce the peak cooling power demand of a building thus reducing the size of air conditioning equipment and period for which it is generally required. A passive cooling technique encompasses a number of methods of natural insulation, heat rejection, ventilation and heating/cooling of space using constant temperature inside earth.

During building design, it is important that the building design team is provided with information based on various transient physical processes, as it will be necessary to have them quantified, whenever decisions relating to temperature or energy are required. Progress with the prediction relating to temperature or energy are required. Progress with the predication of energy consumption has occurred through method, which simulates or models the transient thermal environment in an around building. There is wide variety of techniques, which have been developed to provide solutions to the relatively complex equations expressing continuously changing parameters having phase lag with their end effects. These techniques have been incorporated into many computerized models, which simulate the thermal performance of the buildings.

Evaluating the indoor climate and energy conditions as well as the designing of heating, cooling and ventilating plants requires calculation on complex building with several thermal zones and rooms. In this process the buildings id divided into thermal zones for dynamic simulations. Any programme normally needs information about materials, equipments, occupancy, usage system with detail description of building component.

An appropriate shading device can effectively reduce the variation of the outdoor weather so as to provide an acceptable indoor-climate. While reporting the result of full scale laboratory experiments carried out in Israel, Givoni (1976), produced the following results:

i. External shading devices are much more efficient than the internal shading device.s the elevation the maximum of the indoor temperature above the outdoor temperature were 5.5 and 4.5°C repeating for green and white venation blinds, while with external shading the elevation were 1.8 and 1.2°C respectively.

ii. The color of the shades has considerable effect on the performance using external and internal shades. Light coloured internal shades are sent to be more effective.

iii. Efficient external shade3 can reduce the 90% heating effect of solar radiation, while an inefficient internal shade would reduce only 20-25% of solar heating effects.

Studies on energy conversation for building have been conducted for more than a decade. Records of standard meteorological information's are available. A number of ground station have facilities for beam diffuse and global radiation measurements. The recent study conducted by US-ASEAN buildings includes evaluation of the OTTV (over all thermal transfer value) of buildings. A simulation tool DOE-2 was also introduced to ASEAN through this programme. Also useful is a load-profile study conducted by the distribution electric utility. Customer load profiles are recorded, typically over 7 days, and results grouped according the standard classification. The buildings details were coded for DOE-2simulaton. Whole buildings, whole year energy calculations were performed. The DOE-2 programme automatically sizes the cooling equipment. It also reports resulting space temperature and simulate running chillers according to a preprogrammed sequence. If the use specified chillers are under size or inadeque chillers capacities are specified, DOE-2 reports temperatures rises in the conditioning spaces.

In another study of Saudi Arabia where oil is cheap, the electricity is fairly inexpensively about 3 kWh (Sayigh 1976b). Electrical equipment, say Freon window type air conditioners, will cost about \$60 per month per family while mechanical draught cooling tower or desert cooler will cost about \$30 per month family. An average a department or home requires 1.5m^3 of water per day. Using an open pond or a tray of water with a surface area of 50m^3, and since the average rate of evaporation during the summer month in Riyadh is 300 mm per month or say 10 mm per day, the amount of exported water will be 0.5 m^2. During the November meeting of COMPLES 1975, in Dhahran, the proposed a house with night cooling that water as storage and has a ground area of 100 m^2. By means of such cooling, the rise in temperature with regard to night temperature is only 1.56°C can be tolerated. The calculations were made for 6-mm glass occupying the whole of the external wall and when necessary, light coloured internal blinds were used. A heat transfer coefficient of 5.7 W/m2 °C was taken for the convective heat flow between the internal surface of the glass and the surface of the blind to the room air. The radiant coefficient for heat transfer between the blinds and glass was taken as 5.7 W/m^2 °C. The solar intensities used in the calculation were derived from data prepared at BKS and the values used are direct radiation uniform background intensity is assumed for diffuse radiation.

In a study conducted in Thailand, the energy saving potential for office equipments including personal computer (PCs) System printers, Copies and facsimile machine has been presented. The field surveys were under taken to assess the energy consumption in commercial buildings. The load pattern were monitored to determine the times spent in active standby, suspends and off modes. These data were combined with estimated diversity factors and power measurement in each mode to find the annual energy saving potentials. Idle losses are 53% for PC system, matrix and inject printers, 98% for laser printer and 98% for fax machines. Office equipment accounts for only 2.2-5.6% of total energy consumption in building audited; up to 25% of this energy consumption can be saved without extra cost. If all commercial buildings in Thailand have similar use pattern annual energy consumption and commercial peak-demand saving will be of the order of 700GWh and 200 MW respectively, by the year 2005.

We present an international profile of activities and research issues related to energy consumption for buildings. The past decades, a few cross-nation comparative studies have been published that address energy standards for residential buildings in industrialized countries. Over last decade, improved in calculation methods, computer modeling and buildings, energy research have provided the means for many countries to reduces their original standards and develop more comprehensive versions. Many countries without energy standards have gathered energy consumption data that could support their developments. Audits of government office building in India suggest that 33% of electricity use in a typical buildings could be saved through management and technological changes with an average payback time of 9 month similarity estimates from former Soviet Union suggest that 25% of the energy used in existing building could be saved and up to 50% in new buildings.

The study of solar energy for use in residential heating and cooling has been done on only a very limited basis. Previous work is more substantial in area of solar energy use for house heating (usually accompanied with use in providing service hot water). Quite a few solar energy houses have been constructed. For example MIT has been studying solar houses for a number of years and Engebretson [12] summarizes the operation of the fourth and lost house for the years of 1959 and 1960. The performance of this house was felt to be satisfactory with no major problems encountered. Actual cost figures were not presented, however it was believed that the fairly large additional cost of solar energy components is being reasonably offset by the savings in fuel cost.

An experimental system, which provides heating and cooling for a house in Tueson, Arizona was studies by Bliss. This house and solar energy is not the type hot would prove economically feasible for wide scale use, since its last is quite large, however, as pointed out by the author the house is constructed for main purpose of studying the conversion and use of solar energy for residential heating and cooling. Hose cooling is accomplished by circulation of cool water through the house. This water is cooled by, radiative cooling of night (by circulation through roof panels) and the operation of heat pump which transfer energy from one section of tank to another. The presence of a quality of hot water and a quality of cool water allows favourable characteristics of being able to provide heating and cooling inter changeably. The circulation of cool water, however, does not allow for dehumidification of the room air and it this system was to be used in a more humid climate than the Tueson site, a dehumidifier would need to be added to the system.

Another variation of solar energy home is presented by Thomason and Thomason [..], which uses a simple type of solar collector and energy storage by means of large water tanks, which is surrounded by a layer of stones. A number of such houses have been studied and the claims to the costs involved with these houses are quite impressive. The system provides heating and cooling of the house with cooling being only terms of sensible heat removal.

Most of early work in the field of solar energy for residential use was summarized in a report of proceeding of symposium held in 1950 at MIT[12]. Presentation of collector models and system models at this symposium are still being used to day.

One of the earlier computer studies of house heating by use of solar energy was made by Buchbery and Roulet (ii). Equations modeling a solar energy system were used with hourly weather bureau data to accomplish the simulation. One of their conclusion was that a maximum collector cost of 115/ft^2 was allowable competitiveness of the solar energy system, which provided heating and service hot water.

One of the earlier mentioning of solar heating and cooling was made by LOF [20] in 1955 in which we discussed the use of triethyl glocol for dehumidification of air. In a more recent pager Tybout and LOF [10] discuss the results of computer simulation of house heating for various sites in the United States. Equations using eight design parameters were used to describe the system and holy weather burea data as employed for use on a digital computer.

2.1 Energy conservation options in buildings

In principle, the thermal comfort of buildings deals with the flux into the building envelop through building materials. The thermal design of a building for efficient heating and cooling integrates a large number of factors that affect the energy balance and hence the energy conservation. The factors that influence the thermal behavior of the buildings are: (i) solar space conditioning (ii) day lighting and ventilation and (iii) embodied energy through building materials. This section presents literature review and the significance of thermal performance of buildings.

2.1.1 Solar space conditioning in buildings

The solar energy reaching the earth is far more in excess to the total energy demand of the world. Solar space conditioning is challenging because of the multi dimensional approach to achieve the human comfort in the building envelope. The literature indicates extensive research on various, space conditioning options as discussed by Duffie and Beckman (1991); Sodha et al (1986); Kaushik et al (1089); Sujit (1994); Bharadwaj (1998), Bansal et al (2001).

The literature suggests two systems of solar space conditioning of buildings active and passive systems [Sodha et al., (1986), Bansal and Cook (2001)]. Conventional approach of solar heating of buildings incorporate separate collector and separate thermal storage. The thermal energy is transported from the storage to building thermal control system in a regulated way using air or liquid as a heat transport liquid. This is known as ***active solar heating system***. This system obviously required ancillary equipment in the form of heat exchanger, fans etc and it is also essential to have proper maintenance regularly. However, the literature also indicates that although the active solar heating of buildings is capable enough to provide thermal comfort, it is complex in operation and expensive in installation. On the contrary, passive heating system has no separate collector and the structure of the building works as a natural solar collector. Thus, the building envelope is one of the important items to be considered initially for exploring all possibilities to reduce the thermal load of the buildings. Therefore, before considering the active solar conditioning system, it is essential to study and analyze the building components and its thermal behavior to bring the thermal comfort inside the building envelope.

A *passive solar design* is equivalent to a 'live in' solar collector with a profound impact on architectural design and lifestyle of the occupants. This is an inbuilt character of the building, which includes the building elements that admits, absorbs, stores and releases solar energy. Thus it reduces the need of auxiliary energy for comfort heating and cooling. The passive design can be classified broadly into direct gain, indirect convective loops, and thermal storage components of roof/walls. Direct gain for passive space heating system is considered as simplest of all passive systems. The simple physics of this heating system is that sunlight penetrates into a highly insulted room with a heavy interior structure through south facing window.

In order to avoid over heating during the day and cooling at night, the floor and wall must be constructed of materials capable of storing heat for using at night. The commonly used materials are masonry and water. In *passive solar options*, the relationship between glazing and thermal mass influences the interior temperature fluctuations of the buildings.

Building design and specifications are important as it can minimize the solar heat gains in the summer. Similarly, the heating can be met by allowing storing desired quantity of radiation of heating during the winter. Building components i.e. roof, walls and floors may be designed to have desired insulation to avoid the excess heat penetrating into the building evelope.

There is no substitute for good energy conserving architectural design, which optimizes the solar gains in the building. The conventional active methods of heating and cooling of buildings are different from that of natural passive means. Proper design and desired buildings specifications of building components at the early stages of the design process can effectively help in achieving thermal comfort with minimum dependence upon HVAC system and with minimum energy requirements.

There is no substitute for good energy, conserving architectural design, which optimizes the solar gains in the buildings. The conventional active methods of heating and cooling of buildings are different from that of natural passive means. Proper design and desired building specifications of buildings components at the early stages of the design process can effectively help in achieving thermal comfort with minimum dependence upon HVAC system and with minimum energy requirements.

Building elements consist of more than one material. A typical masonry wall or RCC roof has a plaster on either side of the surface. Especially, the exposed side of the roof/wall shall have various waterproofing or terracing treatment layers above it.

Air to air thermal conductance takes into account the resistance between building element surfaces and the surrounding air and are the useful measures of the heat transfer conducted by th building element under steady state conditions i.e. when the temperature on both sides of the element remain constant. However, if the building elements are subjected to temperature fluctuations, not only the heat transmitted by the element but also the time taken for heat to travel through the element becomes important.

A fluctuating temperature wave outside the building element, gives rise to another temperature wave with lower amplitude inside the buildings. The temperature waves are out of phase by an angle called time lag, which depends upon the thermal diffusivity and thickness of the building layer.

Massive building elements such as brick walls and roof with terracing have a larger time lag. Accordingly, it may increase the temperature levels at the time of non-sunshine hours. This may provide the comfort conditions especially in the heating period when the outside temperature is low, whereas it may facilitate less temperature in the sunshine hours, which may bring certain amount of comfort conditions in the cooling periods. Thus, it calls for studying various combinations of building materials for walls, roof and terracing to appreciate the thermal conditions of the building envelope to achieve the balance between the affordable discomforts to acute discomfort.

Thermal storage system due to its significant relevance in passive solar heating and cooling has been addressed in a number of experimental, analytical and numerical studies [Kaushik et al (1994)]. There are many standardized concepts of passive solar heating using various storage options as given by Francis (1984). However, only a few relates to underground options [Diner (1987);Sodha et al (1992), Chandra et al, (2000)].

he concept of using buried pipes or underground tunnels as 'heat exchangers' is seen in Islamic or Persian architecture. Besides, isolated cases can also be traced back to several centuries in Europe, where natural caves and tunnels were employed for cooling the homes of wealthy Romans. Similar, though rare, examples have also been found elsewhere in southern Europe as well as Asia.

In India too, subterranean structures have been in vogue since ancient times [Sharma et al (1989)]. However, properly designed man made systems are of a much more recent origin. What commenced with the digging of a system of underground tunnels has since been modified with the laying of pipes made of plastics, cement, and corrugated metal to obtain desirable results. Hendrick (1980) studied the experimental and theoretical performance of such earth-tube heat exchanger systems and presented some performance data. Interestingly, actual performance data appeared close to the theoretically calculated values.

Francies (1984) carried out more rigorous studies in the US. In this experiment, an earth tube cooling system, consisting of two plastic tubes (diameter 0.20 m, length 120 m and buried at a depth of 3 m), was installed in a house at Illinois. In France, the different uses of an earth heat exchanger in buildings were explored by Trombe et al (1994); such as saving in house energy consumption by preheating fresh air in winter, avoiding freezing risk in dwellings during winter, refreshing air and improving comfort conditioning in summer. Their systems keep the indoor air temperature under 27⁰C and keep away the need for a conventional air conditioning system.

In India, Sodha et al (1985) reported the experimental performance of an existing large earth air tunnel system under a hospital complex in Mathura (UP). Recent applications of the system include residential buildings, small commercial buildings, animal pens, henhouses, and greenhouses as it has dynamic potential to conserve the energy.

The percentage of energy stored depends upon the size and distribution of the thermal mass. Bansal and Singh (1985) considered the effect of storage in the form of a concrete slab/water or placing the storage media under the floor. The properly sized thermal storage in the floor can meet significant heating requirement. Sodha et al (1992) analyzed the thermal performance of room coupled to an evaporation cooled storage tank for heating. A novel way of providing the storage tank in the floor of a non air-conditioned building for cold winter climate in Leh (India) was proposed by Bharadwaj (1998).

The energy analysis of the building requires in depth knowledge of the heat flow in buildings. The heat flows in to the building through conduction, convection and radiation, can be represented in a mathematical form using heat transfer processes, which are interrelated, it is essential to apply simultaneous solution technique if the performance predication is to be made temporal and /or spatial [Chandra and Puri (2000)].

Analyzing the heating and cooling load of a building exposed to solar radiations is an important requirement in thermal design of building. The basic reason for necessity of the time dependent heat flow analysis is that the time constant for temperature variations in the building is of the same order as the time constant for the climatic changes [Kaushik et al (1982)].

Although some numerical methods such as finite difference, electrical analogue and response factor methods are available in the literature, the actual time dependent behavior of a building can be assessed explicitly from the analytical model, which includes the periodic variations of solar intensity and ambient air temperature (Givoni, 1991). This model is based on several assumptions such as identical materials and same thickness, the thermo physical properties of walls/roof are constant and homogeneous and heat transfer coefficients are constant for heating and cooling periods. The literature [Kaushik et al (1982); Puri 986] also indicates that the temperature of the ground is moderately constant after the depth of 4 m. The natural behavior of the ground has been integrated with the earth air tunnel for achieving the comfortable thermal conditions in the building envelope [Singh (1994)].

The performance of an earth air tunnel heat exchanger system also depends upon the ground temperature and moisture distribution as well as on the ground surface conditions. Sodha et al (1985), conducted extensive experimental investigations on existing earth air tunnel system for the summer and winter seasons.

2.1.2 Day Lighting and Ventilation

Utilization of daylight in buildings may result in significant saving in electricity consumption for lighting while designing the good quality indoor environment. The concept of dynamic building envelope technologies introduces a potential for higher quality systems aim to increase daylight levels and improves the daylight uniformity within the space, while controlling sunlight by window sizing and reducing glare by window placement [Lorenz (2000)]. Simultaneous control of electric lighting systems and building envelope conventional components can minimize energy use. Predictive control algorithms, can determine the optimal operation of all HVAC system components and building envelope systems in order to achieve annual minimization of energy consumption (due to lighting/heating/cooling) while maintaining good human comfort [McHugh (1995)].

The literature on natural ventilation by thermal buoyancy is available from a conceptual point of view, and the same has been described by Andersen (1999). The factors such as the column, fan speed and pressure head lead to different results, which over estimates the ventilation capacity [Foster and Down (1987). Hence, with reference to the available theoretical equations [Andersen (1995); Nielsen (1992)] there is a need to analyze the temperature difference due to the thermal buoyancy and to integrate it to the thermal model of the buildings. This would analyzes the indoor thermal conditions of the building in a better manner.

Sizing of the openings is one of the important design parameters for ventilation and utilization of day lighting. Window opening are designed to establish a visual link of surroundings and to contribute in adequate day light illumination requirement for different functional spaces of the building. The Ancient Greeks developed the entire cities with the organized feature for all built up areas to have equal access to the sun. day lighting is an energy efficient strategy that allows one to offset the electrical lighting needs with day lighting [Bansal (1999),McHugh (1995)]. It is essential to analyze the available daylight and to utilize it effectively in the buildings for different functional spaces. An analysis of the important factors of the exterior environment, interior environment and fenestration is essential to the beginning of the design process. Each opening placed in the exterior wall of a building should be evaluated in terms of its total impact on the interior environment and the human occupants.

The decision to place fenestration in a building should not be based on arbitrary, superficial reasoning. The sizing of the windows varies from room to room, depending on the function of the room and its orientation. Once the day requirement is fixed with respect to the function of the room, the size, proportion and placement of the opening must be decided with reference to the requirement of day light factor. The sizing of the window must be designed and calculated with reference to the thermal impact of the opening and daylight potential.

The proportions and placements of openings should be based on the quality and quantity of the daylight entering the space. The exterior environment produces and influences the daylight that becomes the source of light for interior daylight calculations. The constantly changing exterior environment is the main feature in the analysis of daylight resources like sun, the sky and ground.

The sky luminance is a function of cloud cover, thus it is termed as over cast sky or clear sky luminance and the light reflected from the ground depends on the reflectance property of the ground cover. In literature several researchers developed different daylight models [BIS (1989); IES (1984); CIE (1973); and Chandra (1996)] to calculate the availability of daylight.

Thereafter, calculation of illumination levels inside a building can be made with respect to the day light factors, internal reflected components and external reflected component and maintenance considerations of the window glazing. In this regard, BIS (1989) has developed user-friendly tables to calculate the indoor illumination levels on the working plane with respect to the opening sizes. The illumination levels of different proportions of window and placement in different locations can present desirable solutions for different functional requirement of the indoor space.

2.1.3 Energy in Building Materials

In building design processes, the specifying of the building materials is one of the vital parameter of functional and structural aspects of the building [Walker et al, (2000)]. Considerable amount of energy is spent in the manufacturing of various building materials. Conservation of energy through building materials becomes important in context of limiting of green house gases emission into the atmosphere and reducing the cost of materials. It is an important area to focus certain issues pertaining to embodied energy in buildings particularly in Indian context.

In recent years, awareness of environmental aspects has grown in buildings and construction sector. Several authors and scientists aimed to reduce the energy consumption at source level i.e. at manufacturing stage. Reddy et al. (2001) conducted extensive research in the field of embodied energy of common and alternative materials. Manufacturing process of building material contributes greenhouse gases emission into the atmosphere causing adverse environmental impacts. Energy requirements for production and processing of different building materials and the CO2 emissions and the implications on environment have been considered by Buchanam and Honey (1994); Suzki et al (1993); Oka et al (1995); and Debnath et al (1995) among others. These studies pertain to New Zealand, Japan and India.

The selection of building materials and technologies for the building construction satisfy the user without causing any adverse impact on environment [Mullick (1993)]. Minimizing the consumption of conventional materials by using alternative materials, methods and techniques can result in scope for considerable energy savings [Reddy, 2001].

Considering the same it is required to identify the energy efficient materials to cut down the consumption of the commercial energy and to work out the appropriate energy efficient materials with specific reference to locally available materials to conserve the energy in building industry. This research also becomes vital from the perspective of estimating embodied energy in alternative building materials and comparison of embodied energy for selecting less energy intensive materials.

2.2 Analysis on non-air conditioned buildings

Most of the literature available on periodic heat transfer is restricted to air-conditioned buildings where the room temperature is constant. Most of the earlier studies on the passive solar buildings have relevance only for air conditioned buildings. However, in general buildings are non air conditioned and the variable parameter is indoor air temperature rather than the heating/cooling load of the building. The thermal design of a non air conditioned building for efficient heating/cooling embraces a large number of factors that effect the energy balance and hence energy consumption.

Kaushik et al (1982) had presented an investigation on thermal behavior of non air conditioned building with variable indoor conditions and the walls and roof being exposed to the periodic solar radiations and atmospheric air. Bharadwaj (1998) analyzed the several storage options of buildings such as concrete storage over ground in the floor, thermal trap storage in floors, water tank storage in the floor analyzed with respect to the above model. Majority of analysis were limited to several simple assumptions including homogenous components and materials.

2.2.1 Need for simultaneous solution in ground heat and mass transfer analysis

The performance of an earth air tunnel heat exchanger system depends upon the ground temperature and moisture distribution as well as on the ground surface conditions. Various simplified models presented in the literature, report a reasonable prediction of extracted air temperature. However, these models are characterized by limited scope of assumptions, as they do not consider the latent heat transfer between air and pipe wall and hence cannot predict the humidity variations of tunnel air. Non-inclusion of latent heat not only affects energy balancing but also limits the scope of determining comfort conditions of the building significantly. Furthermore, most of the models ignored heat transfer phenomenon in the earth, both sensible and latent heat transfer, or considered an axially symmetric heat flow (Bharadwaj, 1998; Tzaferis, 1992) into the ground with constant pipe wall temperature. Constant wall temperature excludes any possibility of determining the long term dynamic performance of an earth air tunnel system.

2.2.2 Storage options in buildings

Available literature does not address the conventional building storage options. The conventional options considered for thermal appreciation in building envelope is of important value as an indicator in general and guiding yardstick to cost effective building design in particular.

However, the commonly available materials are only good enough to provide the comfort conditions in the buildings for cooling period but the results of the heating period demand to explore some other options of bring comfort conditions such as underground storage options. There are various possible configurations of solar heat storage exchangers that could provide a wide range of performance for thermal comforts. Givoni (1991) studied and presented several advantages of under ground thermal storage options for passive heating and cooling of buildings. There is a no significant variation in temperature with time beyond certain depth from the ground surface. Hence, it is possible to stratify the rock bed medium using ground as insulation and storage. The air can be recycled in to the building for heating in the winter as solar energy is not sufficient the rock bed serves the purpose of storing heat energy owing to a higher temperature at a depth below the ground surface. Various storage configurations need to be explored in detail.

2.2.3 Inadequate coverage on windows design in thermal comfort analysis

In developing countries, the settlements dominated by the non air conditioned buildings, these buildings are basically designed to have adequate openings to establish proper cross ventilation to provide respite thermal conditions to the users. Especially, in climatic zones of 'hot and humid' and 'hot and dry' the windows are used to contribute desirable conditions to thermal comfort of the building. However, very limited studies are available in the literature to work out the contributory design parameters of windows in thermal comfort conditions of buildings. Window sizing is quite desirable both from the point of view of natural ventilation and dry lighting.

2.3 Lack of comparative analysis in embodied energy

There is a need to identify and prepare comparative energy estimates to workout the embodied energy consumption in the building design process and materials of construction. It is felt essential and necessary to work out the relation between the cost of materials and the energy consumption to present the economic feasibility for designing the energy efficient buildings. It is required to explore the conventional practices related to local materials by distinguishing the potentialities in term of energy conservation.

Thus by and large, the literature on the passive solar buildings has relevance only for air conditioned buildings. However, in general, buildings are non air conditioned and the variable parameter is indoor air temperature rather than the heating/cooling load of the building. The thermal design of a non air conditioned building for efficient heating/cooling embraces a large number of factors that effect the energy balance and hence energy consumption. Further, an effective utilization of day lighting is the direct reduction in the use of electrical lighting. Similarly, it is known that the enormous energy consumed in the production of building materials, so as to conserve the energy it is required to identify the less energy intensive materials for building design process.

Considering the gray areas of the research for thermal comfort in buildings (as discussed earlier), this research attempts to address them comprehensively. The scope of the research is limited to the following:

A thermal model for predicting the indoor temperature in buildings is developed using passive solar heating/cooling concepts with reference to building components and materials. Besides, the proposes various underground configurations for attaining desirable thermal conditions in the building envelope. These analysis the potentiality of under ground earth air tunnel to achieve the thermal comfort conditions of buildings. This research deals with the components and integrates one parameter to another and optimizes the overall solution in order to achieve the design tools for energy efficient buildings.

- This research is analysis a solar thermal model considering the feasible and local materials for selected major building components i.e. wall, roof and terracing for thermal comfort to bring the indoor temperature to desirable conditions and conserve thermal energy. Thus, the different specifications/configurations of roof/walls i.e. conventional brick masonry, cavity in wall masonry, rat trap bond masonry, stone cladding brick masonry and hollow cement block have been combined with roof terracing options such as normal terracing on conventional RCC slab, lime concrete terracing, mud phuska [1 (clay); 1 (cow dung)] terracing, earthen pot cum mud phuska terracing and ceiling insulation have been integrated in proposed typologies coupled with solar thermal modeling of a non air conditioned building in order to appreciate the space conditioning options.

- Analysis of feasibility of under ground storage system for different design configurations. The potential under ground storage system has been analyzed for different design configurations by developing thermal model with finite difference method to simulate the desirable design configuration of a storage system for thermal comforts.
- Theoretical analysis of window sizing through thermal buoyancy and day lighting in the building with reference to the temperature difference is and coupled to the solar model of a building to determine the indoor temperature. Several day lighting models have been studied to identify a suitable model for determining the design sky and with reference to BIS, the illumination contours have been prepared for different configurations of openings.
- Appreciation of embodied energy profile in buildings with reference to available/local materials. Three building cases with three possible options of material specifications have been studied in this research to ascertain the less energy intensive options to conserve energy. The individual major components such as walls, roofing, terracing plastering, flooring and mortar mixes have been analyzed with different options of less energy intensive materials.

The concepts and an overview of the current state of art in the field of energy conservation in buildings through various components and materials and importance of energy conservation in the building industry. The chapter also presents the significance of the research from the perspective of changing energy consumption situation in the country and analysis of thermal performance of buildings. The chapter also presents the grey areas of research related to thermal comfort analysis and establishes the scope of this research.

There are many studies of thermal design in vernacular architecture has pointed out it is not sufficient to have a qualitative understanding of such buildings. To develop confidence in the natural heating and cooling methods we need data to know the kind of temperatures and thermal environment that prevails in vernacular buildings. Combined with the pattern of building usage, such data can be an indicator of the level of thermal comfort that was provided by the buildings in question.

2.4 Energy Conservation in Ancient Building of Rajasthan

Energy efficient building construction is an important aspect in the Greed Building concept. Masonry buildings are common in thar desert. Thar desert has peculiar weather in Hot and Dry Arid Zone. Normal human comfort demand large amount of energy to maintain appropriate environment. Energy efficiency through use of low energy material product, planning of building, construction and design techniques, operative precautions can make it possible. Certain aspects in this regard are presented with suitable examples.

A Green building should create delight when entered, serenity and health when occupied and regret when departed Perhaps this is one of the most inspiring definitions (CII) of a Green building, articulated in the book 'Natural Capitalism'. The appearance of a GreenBuilding will be similar to any other building. However, the difference is in the approach, which revolved round a concern for extending the life span of natural resources, provide human comfort, safety and productivity. This approach results in reduction in operating costs like energy and water, besides several intangible benefits. Some of the salient features of a GreenBuilding are:

- Minimal disturbance to landscapes and site condition
- Use of recycled and environmental friendly building materials
- Use of non toxic and recycled / recyclable material
- Efficient use of water and water recycling
- Use of energy efficient and eco friendly equipment
- Use of renewable energy
- Indoor air quality for human safety and comfort
- Effective controls and building management system

The energy savings could range from 25-40% depending on the extent of green specifications. Many new materials and services have been introduced as a result of this movement. Some of these materials and equipments include high performance glass, wall and roof insulation, low VOC paints, adhesives & sealants, CRIP certified carpets, FSC certified wood, high albedo roofing material, fly ash blocks, eco-friendly chemicals waterless urinals, high CoP chillers, CO_2 sensors, root zone treatment plants, wind towers. The market potential of green building materials and equipment is estimated to be about Rs 15000 crores by 2010.

A few green materials and equipment are available in the country. To name a few fly ash cement, fly ash block, recycled aluminum, recycled steel, recycled tiles, low VOC paints, bamboo based products, HFC based high efficiency chillers, building controls,, green roof recycled wood etc. However there is a huge market for green materials, which is still untapped. Typical examples are composting toilets waterless urinals, low VOC adhesives & sealants, CRI certified carpets, FSC certified wood, high albedo roof paints, BIPV, CTI certified cooling towers, living machines etc.

2.4.1 Design of green building

Buildings have major environmental impacts over their entire life cycle. Resources such as ground cover, forests, water and energy are depleted to give way to building. A green building depletes the natural resources to the minimum during its construction and operation. The aim of a green building design is to minimize the demand on non renewable resources, maximum the utilization efficiency of these resources, when in use, and maximize the reuse, recycling and utilization of renewable resources. It maximizes the use of efficient building materials and construction practices, optimizes the use of onsite sources and sinks by bio climatic architectural practices, uses minimum energy to power itself, uses efficiency equipment to meet its lighting, air conditioning, and other needs; maximizes the use of renewable sources of energy, uses efficient waste and water management practices, and provides comfortable and hygienic indoor working conditions. In sum, the following aspects of the building design are looked into in an integrated way in a green building.

- Site planning
- Building envelope design
- Building system design (HVAC) heating ventilation and air conditioning, lighting
- Electrical and water heating
- Integration of renewable energy sources to generate energy onsite.
- Water and waste management
- Selection of ecological sustainable materials (with high recycled content, rapidly)
- Renewable resources with low emission potential, etc.
- Indoor environmental quality (maintain indoor thermal and visual comfort, and air quality)

The relevance of energy efficient building has assumed greater significance in the light of fast depleting energy resources, energy scarcity and environmental pollution hitting an obscene high. The building construction is one of the largest energy consuming sectors. Studies conducted by intergovernmental panel on climate change indicate that in 1990, the residential commercial and institutional building sector consumed 31 per cent (1) of global energy and emitted 1900 mega tones of carbon and by 2050; its share may rise to 38 percent and 3800 mega tones, respectively. In our country, it is estimate that about 25 percent of the total energy demands are due to manufacturing materials required in building construction, while another 30 percent of the total energy demands are due to manufacturing materials required in building construction, while another 30 percent go into the running needs of the building. The ministry of power approximation indicates that 20-25 percent of the total electricity consumed in the government buildings are wasted because of inefficient design parameters of the building, thus resulting in a whopping energy financial loss of about Rs 150 crore a year. Energy is a basic requirement for the existence and development of human life. Primarily, the commercial sources such as fossil fuels (coal, oil and natural gas), hydroelectric power and nuclear power provide the energy needs of a country. The demand for energy is growing at an alarming rate year after year. In general, energy efficiency can be achieved in new buildings through.

Load minimization by incorporation of passive solar techniques in building design, Design of energy efficient lighting and HVAC (heating, ventilation & air conditioning) systems. Use of renewable energy systems to meet a part of the building load and use of low energy materials and methods of construction. The primary function of a building is to provide a comfortable indoor environment. Traditional building of earlier times has many built in architectural features for achieving comfort. A number of passive solar techniques were adopted in vernacular architecture in the various climatic zones. Control of the microclimate around the building was always an important design consideration. For example, in a commercial building, the cooling can be saved by about 26% in a hot and dry climate (like Jodhpur) by adopting appropriate design consideration and operation strategies.

In the developed countries the energy consumption growth rate is only marginally higher compared to the population growth rate. For example, in USA energy consumption is projected to grow at 1.3% while the population growth rate is projected to grow at 0.8%.

In contrast, in developing countries like India population growth grate is expected to grow at 1.3% while the energy consumption rate is expected to grow at 4.3%. This trend would strain the energy sector to a large extent. The construction industry in the country is growing at a rapid pace and the rate of growth is 10% as compared to the world average of 5.2%. Hence, energy efficiency in the building sector assumes tremendous importance. The potential for energy savings is 40-50% in buildings, if energy efficiency measures are incorporated at the design stage. For existing buildings the potential can be as high as 20-25% which can be achieved by implementing house keeping and retrofitting measures. The incremental cost incurred for achieving energy efficiency is 5-8% vis-à-vis conventional design cost and can have an attractive payback period of 2-4 years.

2.4.2 Techniques for energy efficiency

The following envelope measure can be considered

- Select high performance glazing with low U-value, low shading coefficient and high VLT (Visual Light Transmittance)
- Insulate the wall. The options for insulation materials can be Extruded
- Polystyrene, expanded polystyrene (thermacol), glass wool etc.
- Brick wall with air cavity can also significantly reduce the heat ingress
- Hollow blocks, fly ash bricks and autoclaved aerated concrete (AAC) blocks are also good insulators
- The heat ingress through the roof can be as high as 12-15%. Insulating the roof can substantially reduce the heat ingress.
- Consider shading devices for window openings.

The available and affordability of materials/equipment which contribute to energy efficiency is another major challenge. Effective energy management is a process that consists of four steps, which are the same steps that are needed for success in any complex business activity.

- Step 1: Identify all your opportunities
- Step 2: Prioritize your activities rationally
- Step 3: Accomplish your activities successfully
- Step 4: Maintain your activities throughout the life of the facility

A super efficient new house uses only 105 to 30% as much energy as a house of similar size that is built to contemporary standards. The biggest users of energy in house are:

- Air conditioning (in warmer climates)

Next in importance are:

- Refrigeration
- Water heating

The smallest energy users in typical dwellings are:

- Lighting

- Cooking
- Laundry
- Dishwashing
- Electronics

2.4.3 The layout and structure of your house

a. Design a layout that tailors energy usage to your lifestyle

b. Install lots of insulation in the walls, the roof, and exposed floors

c. With frame walls, use plywood exterior sheathing caulked and nailed securely

d. Avoid excessive window and skylight area. Limit glass to locations where will do some good, either for a good view or for day lighting.

e. Install double – or triple pane windows that open easily and close tightly, with good thermal barriers in the frames. A special caution about day lighting and passive solar heating.

f. Install doors that have good insulation and excellent weather sealing.

g. Minimize air conditioning cost by shading all windows.

h. Radically vent the air space above attic and cathedral ceiling insulation

i. In warm climates, make the roof top surface shed heat as effectively as possible.

j. Plant trees around the house in a way that optimize shading and makes your yard beautiful.

2.4.4 The energy using equipment of house

The most important principles

a. Select high efficiency models of all energy using equipment.

b. Turn off heating, cooling, lighting and other energy using equipment when you do not need them.

Heating and cooling efficiently

a. Select heating and cooling systems that are tailored to individual spaces.

b. Install programmable thermostats

c. By a thick, cozy goose down comforter, and turn off the heat at night

d. If your heating equipment burns fuel, draw combustion air from the outside.

e. Install the condensing units of air conditioning equipment in cook, clean locations.

f. Install a quiet, high volume ventilation fan to provide outside air cooling.

g. In a warm climate, install ceiling paddle fans.

h. Mange your windows and ventilation

In the Kitchen

i. Install a high volume range hood, combined with a separate outside air supply to the kitchen.

j. Install your refrigerator and freezer in cool areas that isolate them form heat producing equipment, including the range, water heater, and dishwasher.

k. Get a microwave oven and use it

l. Keep lids on your pots and pans when you cook

m. The frozen food in your refrigerator

Saving water and water heating energy

n. Install separate hot and cold water faucets for all basins, tubs, and showers.

o. Select low flow shower heads with adjustable spray patterns.

p. Select toilets that flush efficiently

q. Install an efficient urinal

r. Select an efficient washing machine

s. Turn down the hot water temperature when the house is vacant

Efficient lighting

t. Use reflective interior colours

u. Install fluorescent lighting in rooms where lights stay on for long periods.

v. Make all light fixtures as efficient as possible.

w. Install motion sensors to control lighting in appropriate locations.

A study on energy efficiency in low cost housing is presented. Planning considered row housing, side and back common walls, mirror image in block of two housing units, clear height of room 3.0m, window size etc. he scheme is considered to be located in Western Rajasthan having hot and dry climate. The results are calculated for different orientations (eight), categories of houses (five), weather conditions (two) and plans (regular and mirror image) i.e. total 1600 cases. North South orientation is considered to be the best option for better heat gain. Energy audit must be carried out while planning a house scheme.

The study revealed that energy conservation can be achieved by solar passive techniques applying basics of geometrical and functional planning. Green house is a building for specific purpose and requires environmental control by artificial means of energy. Various design aspects of a solar passive roof for a green house in arid area are highlighted. Planning of interior is important for energy efficient building. Other aspects are plot, landscape & garden, wall thickness, roof, overhead tank, ventilation and lighting, local conditions and innovative techniques etc.

2.4.5 Examples of energy efficient buildings in Rajasthan

a. *JalorTopkhana (Photo 1,2):* This is well built old structure used as an armory store. In photo 1 nos of domes are seen used for extra height and a way to cut high wind velocity. In photo 1 Dome, pillar, jail and balcony provide shade, ventilation, height and to check high wind velocity.

b. *GadisarLake (Photo 3,4):* Lake in desert is like an oasis. Water bodies present in Thar desert provide comfort to the visitors. Buildings in between lake further enhances this comfort.

c. *Salim Singh Haveli (Photo 5,6):* It is a rare example of heritage building maintained by a family. Top storey provide airy atmosphere with fountain inside. The details of fixtures are a unique feature of the building which are helpful in preventing high wind velocity.

d. *MandorePanchkunda (Photo 7,8):*Know as centopahs i.e. cremation campus, use of local material is prevent energy consuming requirement. Repair of heritage structures is a typical problem where compatibility of new and old material is a big problem.

e. *Mehrangarh Fort (Photo 11,12):* Typical blend of massive and safe/secure structure with provision of numerous windows/jharokha in high level Mahal for adequate ventilation.

f. *Patwonki Haveli (Photo 11,12):* World famous Patwonki Haveli has different features for an architect to study e.g. Wooden roof for thermal comfort and main chowk for central shaft providing ventilation, day light and heat regulator.

g. *Amar Singh ChhatriNagour (Photo 13,14):* Locations near pond provide thermal comfort. Use of traditional water bodies e.g. Baori is typical example even used in present time.

h. *Fort School, Bikaner (Photo 15,16):* Location the centre of city of Bikaner and it is comfortable in summer as well as winter due to large thickness of wall and height of the building.

i. *Junagarh Fort, Bikaner (Photo 17,18):* Location the centre of city of Bikaner and it is made up of a traditional materials of large thickness of wall and height of building which provide lesser temperature in summer as well as natural ventilation and lighting.

j. *Gajner Palace, Bikaner (Photo 19,20):* Location near by Bikaner at Gajner and it is a historical example of ancient building in Bikaner.

Photo 1: Jalore Topkhana Domed Roof

Photo 2: Jalore Topkhana Main Dome

Photo 3: Gadisar Lake Entry View

Photo 4: Building in Gadisar Lake

Photo 5: Salim Singh Haveli Top Storey

Photo 6: Salim Singh Haveli Details

Photo 7: Mandore Panchkunda Wide View

Photo 8: Mandore Panchkunda Repair

Photo 9: Mehrangarh Fort Mahal Jarokha

Photo 10: Mehrangarh Fort Massive, Safe

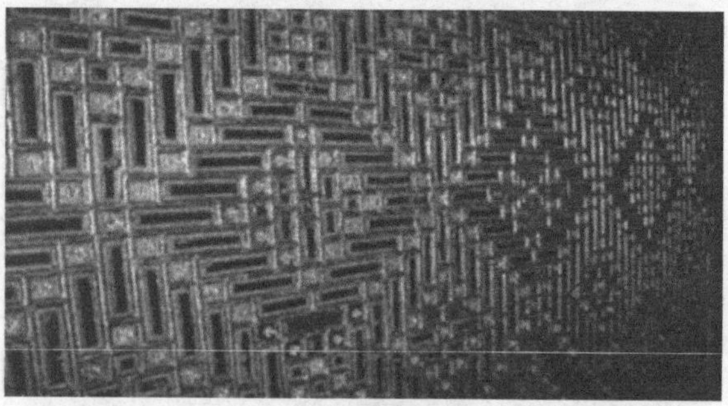

Photo 11: Patwon triki Haveli Wooden Roof

Photo 12: Patwon ki Haveli Main Chowk

Photo 13: Amar Singh Chhatri Naagur

Photo 14: Baori near Amar Singh Chhatri

Photo 15: Front View of Govt. Fort School, Bikaner

Photo16: Inside of Room Govt. Fort School, Bikaner

Photo 17: Front View of Junagarh Fort

Photo 18: Inside View of Junagarh Fort

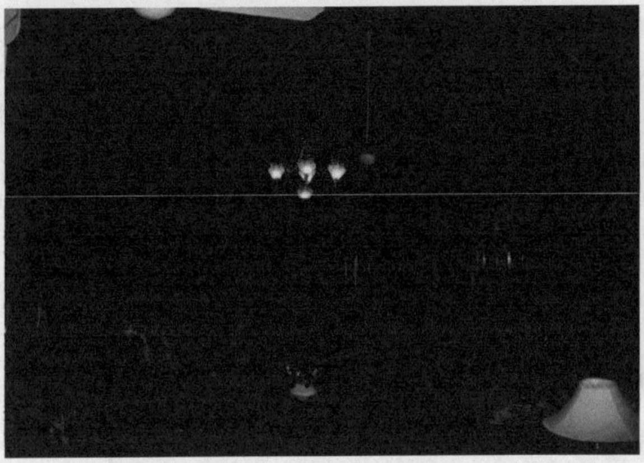

Photo 19:Inside View of Gajner Palace

Photo 20: Front View of Gajner Palace

Fig.2.1: Different ancient building of Rajasthan

3 Simulation Techniques of Energy Conservation In Buildings

3.1 INTRODUCTION

The available computer tools are used to simulate and evaluate the buildings in varying climate conditions. By using these tools a building can be simulated for load calculation with application of different methods for energy conservation in active space conditioning devices under any set of climatic condition. Such tools like POWER DOE, e-QUEST, Energy Plus, Bsim 8000 etc. are very useful for designing and doing cost benefit analysis for various energy conservation options in a purposed building.

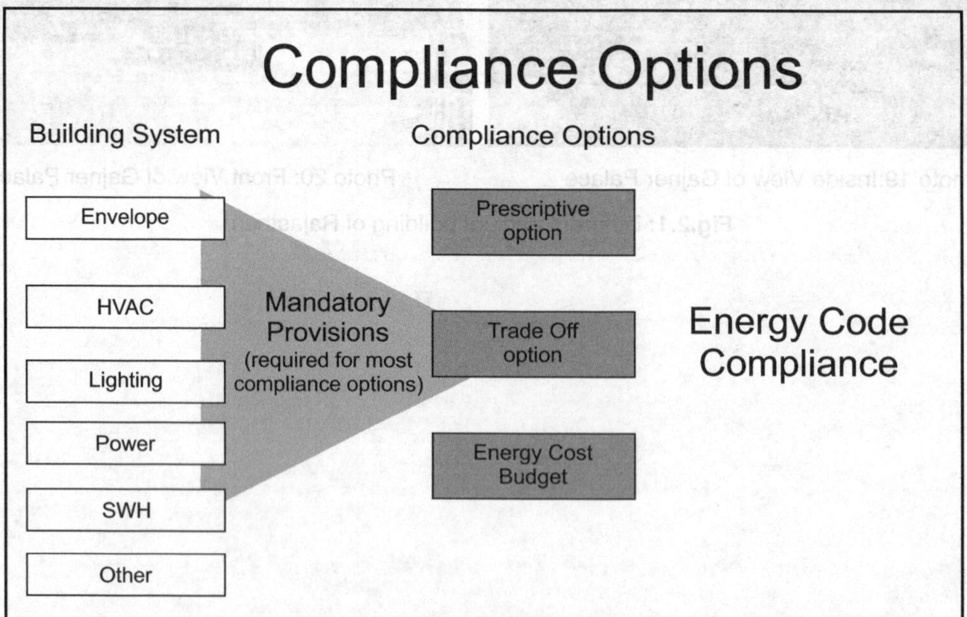

Fig.3.1: Compliance Options

The thermal response of a building many be determined from the heat gain factor through various structural elements viz. wall, window, roof and floor, the internal heat loads, rate of ventilation occupancy schedules and trends etc. The transfer of heat between a building and its environment largely depend upon the overall conductance of structure, the degree of exposure to weather including sunshine and existing temperature differences between inside and outside. Other parameters like wind velocity also effect this value. All of these features can be modeled using heat transfer and mass transfer equations.

In recent years, various mathematical techniques have been developed for modeling heat gain and thermal load in buildings. Various models developed so far can be divided into three basic categories:

- Approximate methods
- Correlation methods
- Analytical methods

Modeling of heat transfer and cooling load requirement is necessary for any building keeping in mind the objectives of minimizing energy consumption for controlling internal environment. Such modeling covers analysis of effect of external environment features such as solar radiation, wind, natural light, moisture and internal sources of thermal load like lighting, ,electrical appliances, occupancy etc.

During building design, it is important that the building design team is provided with information based on various transient physical processes, as it will be necessary to have them quantified, whenever decisions relating to temperature or energy are required. Progress with the prediction of energy consumption has occurred through method, which simulates or models the transient thermal environment in and around building. There are wide varieties of techniques, which have been developed to provide solutions to the relatively complex equations expressing continuously changing parameters. These techniques have been incorporate into many computerized models, which simulate the thermal performance of the buildings.

Evaluating the indoor climate and energy conditions as well as the designing of heating, cooling and ventilating plants requires calculation on complex building with several thermal zones and rooms. In this process the building is divided into thermal zones for dynamic simulations. Any program normally needs information about construction materials, equipment occupancy, usage system with detail description of building component.

3.2 SIMULATION GENERAL REQUIREMENTS

3.2.1 Energy Simulation Program

The simulation program shall be a computer-based program for the analysis of energy consumption in buildings and be approved by the authority having jurisdiction. The simulation program and shall model the following:

a. Energy flows on an hourly basis for all 8,760 hours in the year,

b. Hourly variations in occupancy, lighting power, miscellaneous equipment power, thermostat setpoints, and HVAC system operation, defined separately for each day of the week and holidays,

c. Thermal mass effects,
d. Ten or more thermal zones,
e. Part-load and temperature dependent performance of heating and cooling equipment,
f. Air-side and water-side economizers with integrated control, and
g. All of the standard design characteristics specified in this chapter.

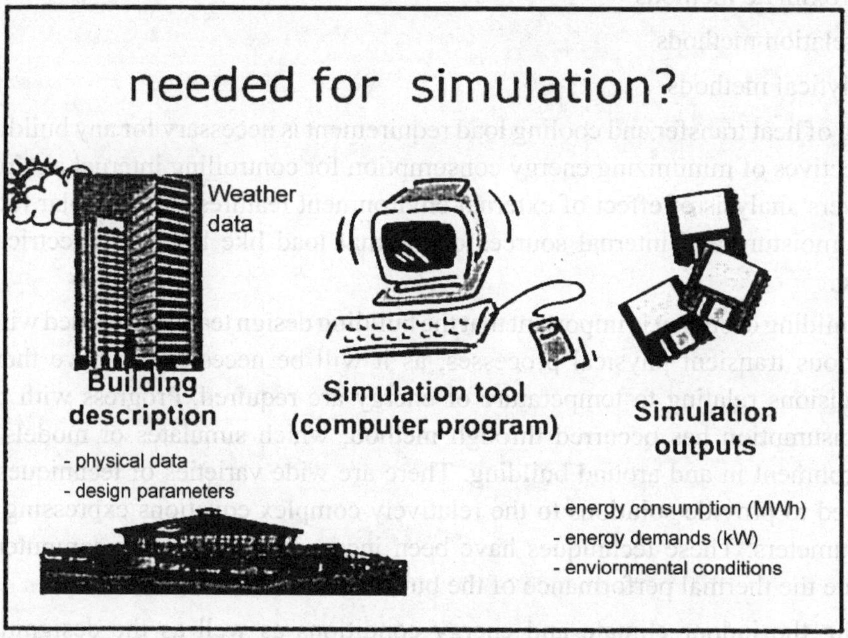

Fig.3.2: Need for Simulation

3.2.2 Climatic Data

The simulation program shall use hourly values of climatic data, such as temperature and humidity from representative climatic data, for the city in which the proposed design is to be located. For cities or urban regions with several climatic data entries, and for locations where weather data are not available, the designer shall select available weather data that best represent the climate at the construction site.

3.2.3 Compliance Calculations

The proposed design and standard design shall be calculated using the following:

a. Same simulation program,
b. Same weather data, and

c. Same building operation assumptions (thermostat setpoints, schedules, internal gains, occupant loads, etc.)

3.3 Bsim2000

It is package of easy to use and flexible progrmms for evaluating the indoor climate and energy conditions as well as the designing of heating, cooling and ventilating plants. The Bsim 2000 package comprise the following programs:

- Sim view (use interface and graphic model editor)
- Tsbi5 (building simulation tool)
- Xsun (dynamic solar and shadow simulation)
- Sim light (day light calculation tool)
- Bv98 (Compliance checker)
- Sim DXF (CAD import facility)

Bsim 2000 permits calculation on complex building with several thermal zones and rooms simultaneously. Bsim 2000 utilizes data from all structure in the thermal evaluation. Bsim 2000 interact directly with other applications for compliance with building regulations, dynamic with results, solar and shadow distribution, CAD import for model making an daylight calculations.

Input: When using the Bsim2000 the building is divided into rooms, some in thermal zones. Only rooms in thermal zones will be simulated dynamically the rest can be used in other applications. The followings groups of information are needed:

- Building materials
- Building component
- Equipments and systems

Output: The user can close any of the calculated parameters for each thermal zone plus data from ambient climate, as output on hourly, weekly, monthly or periodically basis, in either tabular or graphic form. The variables can also be presented in sum graphs or tables. Finally the energy branches for each zones or the whole building can be shown. Outputs can be copied (graphic or numbers) for presentation in other programs.

The analysis of indoor thermal climate in complex buildings or building with special requirements for the indoor climate. There is only problem with this building simulation tool that it is not taking into account the air flow caused by wind pressure on the facades.

The following calculation can be made on the buildings using the Bsim 2000.

- Heat gain from solar radiation, persons, lighting and equipment.
- Solar radiation through window's
- Heating, cooling and ventilation
- Power and energy balance

- Moisture balance
- Temperature conditions
- Heat and air exchange between zones
- Shading conditions
- Variable infiltration and venting
- Several different ventilation systems simultaneously \surface temperature and condensation risks
- Air exchange in connection with infiltration and opening of windows
- Air exchange between rooms
- Heat and refrigeration recovering in ventilation plants
- Supply and exhaust air temperature in ventilation plants
- Power from heating and cooling coils in ventilation plants
- Moistures in ventilation plants
- Control of thermal loss calculations according to national standard of steady state.

3.4 e-QUEST

e-QUEST is a sophisticated, yet easy to use building energy use analysis tool which provides professional level result with a affordable level of effort. This free ware tool was designed to allow you to perform detailed analysis of today's state of the art building design technologies using today's most sophisticated building energy use simulation techniques but without requiring extensive experience in the 'art' of building performance modeling. This is accomplished by combining a building creation wizard creation wizard, an energy efficiency measure (EEM) wizard and a graphical results display module with an enhanced DOE-2 derived building energy use simulation program.

The e-QUEST building creation wizard first request of the most general information about building design and then delves into progressively deeper detail. In all, the building description process comprises 23 data entry steps and each step represented by a 'wizard' screen. At each step of component and system options. Although the building description process can get quite detailed, it is not necessary to complete every single step in the wizard.

e-QUEST offers several graphical formats for viewing simulation results. For instance, we can displays graphs of estimated overall building energy on an annual or monthly basis. We can also compare the performance of alternative building designs. In addition, e-QUEST allow to perform multiple simulations and view the alternative results in side by side graphics. If offers:

- Energy cost estimating
- Day light and lighting system control
- Automatic implementation of common energy efficiency measures

Version 2.0 of e-QUEST provides even more comprehensive analysis compatibility. It allows the advances user to input additional building details to analyze complex buildings. A three dimensional view geometry is available in this version as well as HVAC system diagrams.

3.5 POWER DOE-2

It is the latest version of a wall represented and popular energy simulation program developed over the last 20 years by the US. DOE.

DOE-2 performs an hourly simulation of the buildings design for a one year period. It calculates heating or cooling loads for each hour of the year, based on the factors such as:

- Walls
- Windows
- Glass
- People
- Plug loads
- Ventilation

DOE-2 also simulates the performance of:

- Fans
- Pumps
- Chillers
- Boilers
- Other energy consuming devices

During simulation, DOE also tabulates the buildings projected energy use and uses such as:

- Lighting
- Plug loads (computers, appliances, copiers etc.)
- Heating
- Cooling
- Ventilation

We present an International profile of activities and research issues related to energy consumption simulation for buildings. In the past decades, a few cross-national comparative studies have been published that address energy standards for residential buildings in industrialized countries. Over last decade, improved in calculation methods computer modeling and building energy research have provided the means for many countries to reduce their original standards and develop more comprehensive versions. Many countries without any standards have gathered energy consumption data that could support their developments.

These simulation techniques are comprehensive tools which can be effectively used by architects for cost effective passive building design. This can make a tremendous impact on the energy demands for heating and cooling in the various parts of the country resulting in a substantial saving in the consumed energy.

There are various tools for analyzing performance of building in varying climate conditions. Few of such tools are power DOE, e-Quest, ADMIT, SUNCODE, TRNSYS, ESP, TSB13 and Energy plus. By using these tools buildings can be simulated for load calculation with application of different methods for energy conservation in active space conditioning devices under any set of climatic conditions. Such tools are very useful for designing and doing cost benefit analysis for various energy conservation options in a purposed building.

The concept of buildings merely as a means of shelter has fast been changing to that of a controlled environment wherein the human body is in thermal equilibrium with this environment. Elucidating on the thermal equilibrium a littler further. American Society for Heating Refrigeration and Air-conditioning Engineering (ASHRAE) defined thermal comfort as "that condition of the mind which expresses satisfaction with the thermal environment". Although vernacular structures as evident from various literatures used indigenous techniques for manipulating the internal environment, today with the advent of technologies, this thermal comfort is achieved by the use of mechanical equipment such as convectors, air-conditioners etc. A study of the total global energy consumption reveals that 45% of the energy is used in heating, cooling and lighting of buildings and a further 5% is used in building construction (Tonny Rigg and Ruth Lahav, 1995). A study of the buildings in the United Kingdom shows that for newly designed buildings it is possible to have a 50% reduction in energy consumption through energy efficient building design while for existing buildings a reduction of 25% is possible (Clarke and Maver, 1991). The energy consumption in the Indian building sector, being more subdued, it is expected that the consumption of energy in India and the rest of the developing countries alone is going to increase two fold. Hence, quantification is an important step in this direction. In India energy used for air conditioning of commercial buildings accounts for 32% of the total energy consumption in the commercial sector (Nadel et al., 1991). This can be reduced by applying energy conserving measures in buildings and other systems.

3.6 Energy Budget Method

- Even better than trade-off method
- Included HVAC, lighting and other services
- Based on whole building performance
- Individual components may not comply
- Comparison with standard building on annual energy use basis
- Standard building defined as similar energy efficient building
- Better lighting and HVAC may relax requirements for envelope or vice versa
- Requires energy simulation of proposed building
- Only hourly analysis acceptable

- Output files to be attached with the compliance report
- Procedure is similar to LEED rating system

3.6.1 Data needed for whole building simulation

i. Physical Data: Building, Geometry – Plans, Sections & Elevations Construction Technology: Material – Thermo – Physical

ii. Visual Properties: Color / reflection

iii. Weather Data:

Dry Bulb Temperature	Wet Bulb Temperature
Dew Point Temperature	Relative Humidity
Vapour Pressure	Wind Speed
Wind Direction	Atmospheric Pressure
Rainfall	Cloud Cover
Visibility	Moisture
Total Radiation on Horizontal & Vertical	

iv. Other inputs to the Model

a. Internal Heat Gains
- Lighting in Watts/ft^2
- Plug loads in Watts/ft^2
- People, sensible and latent (moisture) loads

b. Schedules
- Equipment/lighting schedules
- People schedules
- Plug loads schedules

c. Systems
- Cooling system type – source, distribution, terminal units
- Set points (temperature and humidity)
- Ventilation system types
- Fan and pump inputs
- Economizers and / or heat recovery system
- Domestic hot water system

4 Passive System of Energy Conservation in Buildings

4.1 INTRODUCTION

Since the demand for better quality of life is increasing continuously day by day, it has becomes extremely important to find ways for satisfying need of space conditioning with minimum use of scarcely available energy in the country. There are two ways for space conditioning, one is by using active system and second is through use of passive system. An active system requires energy, usually n the form of electricity for its operation whereas passive system works in national way toward maintaining indoor comfort, using a combination of suitable materials, proper orientation of building proper layout with respect to neighboring building, using proper shading devices, using natural lighting, natural ventilation, cooling, energy auditing and energy management etc.

Thus, in order to achieves the large reductions in the utilization of the conventional energy. It is essential to evaluate the appropriate models, methods and strategies to conserve energy through the various building components and materials with an appropriate integration of space conditioning options. It is also important to evolve the indexing tools to guide the building design process. This research assumes significance from the above mentioned perspectives.

4.2 Steady State Heat Gain and Loss Analysis

There are three modes of heat transfer, i.e. conduction, convection and radiation, that occur simultaneously during heat transfer in building components, namely, walls, roof, windows and floor. In addition to these heat transfer modes the building components have certain heat storage capacity. For the sake of completeness, these mechanisms are described briefly below:

4.2.1 Conduction

Heat conduction is a process which takes place only within the material. It involves direct transfer of heat between the neighboring particles of the material. The heat is passed on from one particle to another, and is transferred from the warmer region to colder region. The higher the temperature difference, the larger will be the rate of heat conduction. The rate of heat conducted through a material can be expressed by the following Fourier equation:

$$q = -k\frac{\partial\theta}{\partial x} = \frac{k(\theta_2 - \theta_1)}{L}$$

4.2.2 Convection

Thermal convection is defined as the process of heat transfer from a sold surface to the fluid by the combined action of conduction and mass transfer. Convective heat transfer rates depend upon the velocity and nature of fluid flow. If the fluid movement is taking place due to buoyancy forces arising from density differences cased by temperature gradients, the mode of heat transfer is termed as free or natural convection, whereas the process in which the fluid movement is cased by some external agency, such as a pump or a blower, it is termed as forced convection. The analogy when extended to buildings, solid surfaces could be the wall/roof/floor section while the fluid could be the room air or the ambient air.

The rate at which heat is transferred through convection is defined by a heat transfer coefficient, h_c given by the following equation:

$$q = h_c(\theta_1 - \theta_2)$$

The convective heat transfer coefficient is dependent upon:

— air velocity

— surface and air temperature

— roughness of the surface

— position of the building component (horizontal or vertical)

4.2.3 Radiation

Thermal radiation is the exchange of heat from a body at a higher temperature another body at a lower temperature by the mechanism of electromagnetic wave propagation. The amount of thermal radiation that leaves a surface is not only a function of its temperature, but is also related to its surface property known as emissivity (Rogers and Mathew, 1974). Most building materials, regardless of their colors (including glass), have high emissivity in the far-infrared band (typically 90-95%) and then emit/absorb the impinging radiation equally well for a given surface temperature. The total energy radiated over all wavelengths is given by

$$q = \varepsilon\sigma T^4$$

Where ε is emissivity, σ is Stefan Boltzman constant and T is the absolute surface temperature.

4.2.4 Heat Storage Capacity

All building components and objects inside the building have a certain capacity for storing heat. This means that the building materials absorb heat energy during the process of warming up and release the heat energy during the process of cooling down. The capacity to store heat depends on the mass of the material, hence on the density of the material and its specific heat capacity. Therefore, the building material is an important components for understanding the heat transfer mechanism (Bansal et al., 1994).

Consider a building component, the outer façade of which is exposed to solar radiation and ambient conditions while the inner façade is in contact with indoor conditions i.e. the room (Fig 3.1). Illustrates the possible physical phenomena that occur in an external wall or roof.

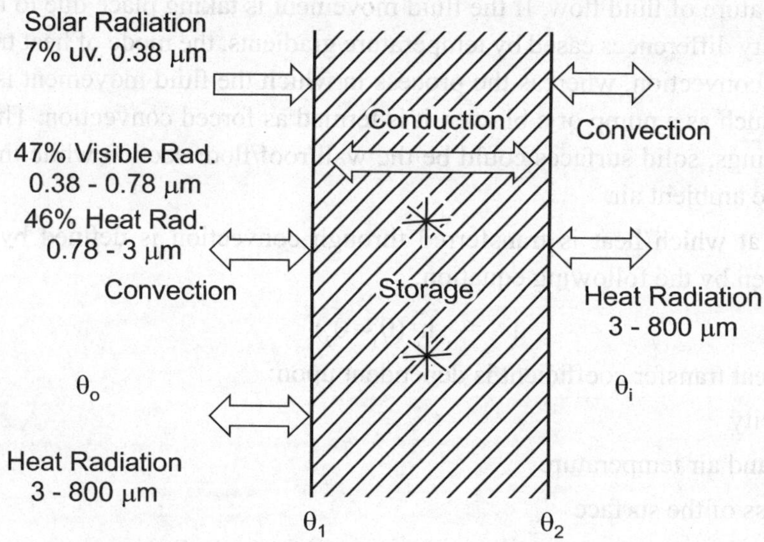

Fig.4.1: Heat transfer mechanism in a building component (Bansal et al., 1994)

The incident solar radiation distribution is essentially in 3 wavelength regions, viz., UV radiation (7%), visible radiation (47%) and heat radiation (46%). The incident radiation when intercepted by the building component is partly reflected and the rest is absorbed by the surface, which increases the temperature of the surface (converted into heat radiation). A part of this absorbed heat radiation is lost to the ambient by convection and radiation while the rest is conduced through the building component. As a result of the thermal storage capacity of the component, which is an inherent property of the building material itself, a part of the conducted radiation is stored in the material while the balance which reaches the inner surface is convicted to the room.

Analyzing the figure in terms of heat gain and heat losses, and considering the temperature of the external surface to be θ_1, the net heat gain at the surface is the sum of the energy absorbed and the convective loss from the surface to the ambient. The equation can be expressed as (the heat transfer is taken from inside to outside):

$$q = -\alpha_s I + h_o(\theta_1 - \theta_o)$$

In the steady state, heat going into the wall is equal to the heat conducted through the wall, and is equal to the heat transfer to the inside surface of wall from the room air i.e.

$$q = \frac{k(\theta_1 - \theta_2)}{L}$$

and $$q = h_i(\theta_2 - \theta_i)$$

Adding yields

$$q \left[\frac{1}{h_o} + \frac{L}{k} + \frac{1}{h_i}\right] = -\frac{\alpha_s I}{h_o} + (\theta_i - \theta_o)$$

or

$$q = \left[\frac{1}{h_o} + \frac{L}{k} + \frac{1}{h_i}\right]^{-1} \left[-\frac{\alpha_s I}{h_o} + (\theta_i - \theta_o)\right]$$

$$= U_w \left[-\frac{\alpha_s I}{h_o} + (\theta_i - \theta_o)\right]$$

$$= Uw\,(\theta_i - \theta_{sa});\ \theta_{sa} = \frac{\alpha_s I}{h_o} + \theta_o$$

Where θ_{sa} is the 'solar temperature'. When the building components (e.g. walls, roof etc.) intercept the solar radiation, there is a rise in the internal temperature. a similar rise in the internal temperature would result if there was no solar radiation but an increase in the external air temperature instead. This increasing external air temperature which produces the same internal temperature rise similarly obtained with the effect of the solar radiation acting in conjunction with the actual external air temperature is termed as solair temperature (Markus and Morris, 1980).

4.3 Energy Conservation Options in Buildings

In principle, the thermal comfort of buildings deals with the heat flux into the building envelope through building materials. The thermal design of a building for efficient heating and cooling integrates a large number of factors that affect the energy balance and hence the energy conservation. The factors that influence the thermal behavior of the buildings are (i) solar space conditioning (ii) day lighting and ventilation and (iii) embodied energy through building materials. This section presents literature review and the significance of thermal performance of buildings.

4.3.1 NATURAL LIGHTING

The lighting requirements in this section shall apply to:

a. Interior spaces of buildings,
b. Exterior building features, including facades, illuminated roofs, architectural features, entrances, exits, loading docks, and illuminated canopies, and,

c. Exterior building grounds lighting that is provided through the building's electrical service.

Exceptions

a. Emergency lighting that is automatically off during normal building operation and is powered by battery, generator, or other alternate power source; and,
b. Lighting in dwelling units.

4.3.2 Mandatory Requirements

4.3.2.1 Automatic Lighting Shutoff

Interior lighting systems in buildings larger than 500 m^2 (5,000 ft^2) shall be equipped with an automatic control device. Within these buildings, all office areas less than 30 m^2 (300 ft^2) enclosed by walls or ceiling-height partitions, all meeting and conference rooms, all school classrooms, and all storage spaces shall be equipped with occupancy sensors. For other spaces, this automatic control device shall function on either

a. A scheduled basis at specific programmed times. An independent program schedule shall be provided for areas of no more than 2,500 m2 (25,000 ft^2) and not more than one floor; or,
b. Occupancy sensors that shall turn the lighting off within 30 minutes of an occupant leaving the space. Light fixtures controlled by occupancy sensors shall have a wall-mounted, manual switch capable of turning off lights when the space is occupied.

4.3.2.2 Space Control

Each space enclosed by ceiling-height partitions shall have at least one control device to independently control the general lighting within the space. Each control device shall be activated either manually by an occupant or automatically by sensing an occupant. Each control device shall

a. Control a maximum of 250 m2 (2,500 ft2) for a space less than or equal to 1,000 m2 (10,000 ft2), and a maximum of 1,000 m2 (10,000 ft2) for a space greater than 1,000 m2 (10,000 ft2).
b. Be capable of overriding the shutoff control required in 7.2.1.1 for no more than 2 hours, and
c. Be readily accessible and located so the occupant can see the control.

Exception to 7.2.1.2(c): The required control device may be remotely installed if required for reasons of safety or security. A remotely located device shall have a pilot light indicator as part of or next to the control device and shall be clearly labeled to identify the controlled lighting.

4.3.2.3 Control in Daylighted Areas

Luminaires in daylighted areas greater than 25 m2 (250 ft2) shall be equipped with either a manual or automatic control device that:

a. Is capable of reducing the light output of the luminaires in the daylighted areas by at least 50%, and
b. Controls only the luminaires located entirely within the daylighted area.

4.3.2.4 Exterior Lighting Control

Lighting for all exterior applications not exempted in 7.4 shall be controlled by a photosensor or astronomical time switch that is capable of automatically turning off the exterior lighting when daylight is available or the lighting is not required.

4.3.2.5 Additional Control

The following lighting applications shall be equipped with a control device to control such lighting independently of general lighting:

a. Display/Accent Lighting. Display or accent lighting greater than 300 m^2 (3,000 ft^2) area shall have a separate control device.
b. Case Lighting. Lighting in cases used for display purposes greater than 300 m^2 (3,000 ft^2) area shall be equipped with a separate control device.
c. Hotel and Motel Guest Room Lighting. Hotel and motel guest rooms and guest suites shall have a master control device at the main room entry that controls all permanently installed luminaires and switched receptacles.
d. Task Lighting. Supplemental task lighting including permanently installed under shelf or under cabinet lighting shall have a control device integral to the luminaires or be controlled by a wall-mounted control device provided the control device complies with 7.2.1.2(c).
e. Nonvisual Lighting. Lighting for nonvisual applications, such as plant growth and food-warming, shall be equipped with a separate control device.
f. Demonstration Lighting. Lighting equipment that is for sale or for demonstrations in lighting education shall be equipped with a separate control device accessible only to authorized personnel.

4.3.2.6 Exit Signs

Internally-illuminated exit signs shall not exceed 5 W per face.

4.3.2.7 Exterior Building Grounds Lighting

Lighting for exterior building grounds luminaires which operate at greater than 100 W shall contain lamps having a minimum efficacy of 60 lm/W unless the luminaire is controlled by a motion sensor or exempt under 7.1.

4.3.3 Interior Lighting Power

The installed interior lighting power for a building or a separately metered or permitted portion of a building shall be calculated in accordance with 7.3.3 and shall not exceed the interior lighting power allowance determined in accordance with either 7.3.1 or 7.3.2.

Tradeoffs of interior lighting power allowance among portions of the building for which a different method of calculation has been used are not permitted.

Exception to 7.3: The following lighting equipment and applications shall not be considered when determining the interior lighting power allowance, nor shall the wattage for such lighting be included in the installed interior lighting power. However, any such lighting shall not be exempt unless it is an addition to general lighting and is controlled by an independent control device.

a. Display or accent lighting that is an essential element for the function performed in galleries, museums, and monuments,

b. Lighting that is integral to equipment or instrumentation and is installed by its manufacturer,

c. Lighting specifically designed for medical or dental procedures and lighting integral to medical equipment,

d. Lighting integral to food warming and food preparation equipment,

e. Lighting for plant growth or maintenance,

f. Lighting in spaces specifically designed for use by the visually impaired,

g. Lighting in retail display windows, provided the display area is enclosed by ceiling-height partitions,

h. Lighting in interior spaces that have been specifically designated as a registered interior historic landmark,

i. Lighting that is an integral part of advertising or directional signage,

j. Exit signs,

k. Lighting that is for sale or lighting educational demonstration systems,

l. Lighting for theatrical purposes, including performance, stage, and film or video production, and

m. Athletic playing areas with permanent facilities for television broadcasting.

4.3.3.1 Building Area Method

Determination of interior lighting power allowance (watts) by the building area method shall be in accordance with the following:

a. Determine the allowed lighting power density from Table 4.1 for each appropriate building area type.

b. Calculate the gross lighted floor area for each building area type.

c. The interior lighting power allowance is the sum of the products of the gross lighted floor area of each building area times the allowed lighting power density for that building area types.

Table 4.1: Interior Lighting Power - Building Area Method

Building Area Type	LPD (W/m^2)	Building Area Type	LPD (W/m^2)
Automotive Facility	9.7	Multifamily	7.5
Convention Center	12.9	Museum	11.8
Court House	12.9	Office	10.8
Dining: Bar Lounge/Leisure	14.0	Parking Garage	3.2
Dining: Cafeteria/Fast Food	15.1	Penitentiary	10.8
Dining: Family	17.2	Performing Arts Theater	17.2
Dormitory	10.8	Police/Fire Station	10.8
Exercise Center	10.8	Post Office	11.8
Gymnasium	11.8	Religious Building	14.0
Healthcare-Clinic	10.8	Retail	16.1
Hospital/Health Care	12.9	School/University	12.9
Hotel	10.8	Sports Arena	11.8
Library	14.0	Town Hall	11.8
Manufacturing Facility	14.0	Transportation	10.8
Motel	10.8	Warehouse	8.6
Motion Picture Theater	12.9	Workshop	15.1

In cases where both a general building area type and a specific building area type are listed, the specific building area type shall apply.

4.3.3.2 Space Function Method

Determination of interior lighting power allowance (watts) by the space function method shall be in accordance with the following:

a. Determine the appropriate building type from Table 4.2 and the allowed lighting power density.

b. For each space enclosed by partitions 80% or greater than ceiling height, determine the gross interior floor area by measuring to the center of the partition wall. Include the floor area of balconies or other projections. Retail spaces do not have to comply with the 80% partition height requirements.

c. The interior lighting power allowance is the sum of the lighting power allowances for all spaces. The lighting power allowance for a space is the product of the gross lighted floor area of the space times the allowed lighting power density for that space.

Table 4.2: Interior Lighting Power – Space Function Method

Space Function	LPD (W/m^2)	Space Function	LPD (W/m^2)
Office-enclosed	11.8	Library	
Office-open plan	11.8	Card File & Cataloging	11.8
Conference/Meeting/Multipurpose	14	Stacks	18.3
Classroom/Lecture/Training	15.1	Reading Area	12.9
Lobby	14	Hospital	
For Hotel	11.8	Emergency	29.1
For Performing Arts Theater	35.5	Recovery	8.6
For Motion Picture Theater	11.8	Nurse Station	10.8
Audience/Seating Area	9.7	Exam Treatment	16.1
For Gymnasium	4.3	Pharmacy	12.9
For Exercise Center	3.2	Patient Room	7.5
For Convention Center	7.5	Operating Room	23.7
For Religious Buildings	18.3	Nursery	6.5
For Sports Arena	4.3	Medical Supply	15.1
For Performing Arts Theater	28	Physical Therapy	9.7
For Motion Picture Theater	12.9	Radiology	4.3
For Transportation	5.4	Laundry – Washing	6.5
Atrium-first three floors	6.5	Automotive-Service Repair	7.5
Atrium-each additional floor	2.2	Manufacturing	
Lounge/Recreation	12.9	Low Bay (<8m ceiling)	12.9
For Hospital	8.6	High Bay (>8m ceiling)	18.3
Dining Area	9.7	Detailed Manufacturing	22.6
For Hotel	14	Equipment Room	12.9
For Motel	12.9	Control Room	5.4
For Bar Lounge/Leisure Dining	15.1	Hotel/Motel Guest Rooms	11.8
For Family Dining	22.6	Dormitory- Living Quarters	11.8
Food Preparation	12.9	Museum	

Laboratory	15.1	General Exhibition	10.8
Restrooms	9.7	Restoration	18.3
Dressing/Locker/Fitting Room	6.5	Bank Office-Banking Activity Area	16.1
Corridor/Transition	5.4	Religions Buildings	
For Hospital	10.8	Worship-pulpit, choir	25.8
For Manufacturing Facility	5.4	Fellowship Hall	9.7
Stairs-active	6.5	Retail	
Active Storage	8.6	Sales Area	18.3
For Hospital	9.7	Mall Concourse	18.3
Inactive Storage	3.2	Sports Arena	
For Museum	8.6	Ring Sports Area	29.1
Electrical/Mechanical	16.1	Court Sports Area	24.8
Workshop	20.5	Indoor Field Area	15.1
Sleeping Quarters	3.2	Warehouse	

Table 4.3: Interior Lighting Power – Space Function Method

Space Function	LPD (W/m2)	Space Function	LPD (W/m2)
Convention Center Exhibit Space	14.0	Fine Material Storage	15.1
		Medium/Bulky Material Storage	9.7
		Parking Garage-Garage Area	2.2
		Transportation	
Airport – Concourse			6.5
Air/Train/Bus – Baggage Area			10.8
Terminal – Ticket Counter			16.1

4.3.3.3 Installed Interior Lighting Power

The installed interior lighting power calculated for compliance with 7.3 shall include all power used by the luminaires, including lamps, ballasts, current regulators, and control devices except as specifically exempted in 7.1.

Exception to 7.3.3: If two or more independently operating lighting systems in a space are controlled to prevent simultaneous user operation, the installed interior lighting power shall be based solely on the lighting system with the highest power.

4.3.3.3.1 Luminaire Wattage

Luminaire wattage incorporated into the installed interior lighting power shall be determined in accordance with the following:

a. The wattage of incandescent luminaires with medium base sockets and not containing permanently installed ballasts shall be the maximum labeled wattage of the luminaires.
b. The wattage of luminaires containing permanently installed ballasts shall be the operating input wattage of the specified lamp/ballast combination based on values from manufacturers' catalogs or values from independent testing laboratory reports.
c. The wattage of all other miscellaneous luminaire types not described in (a) or (b) shall be the specified wattage of the luminaires.
d. The wattage of lighting track, plug-in busway, and flexible-lighting systems that allow the addition and/or relocation of luminaires without altering the wiring of the system shall be the larger of the specified wattage of the luminaires included in the system or 135 W/m (45 W/ft). Systems with integral overload protection, such as fuses or circuit breakers, shall be rated at 100% of the maximum rated load of the limiting device.

4.3.4 Exterior Lighting Power

For building exterior lighting applications specified in Table 4.4, the connected lighting power shall not exceed the specified lighting power limits specified for each of these applications.

Trade-offs between applications are not permitted. Exterior lighting for all other applications (except those included in the Exceptions to 7.4) shall comply with the requirements of 4.4.

Table 4.4 Exterior Building Lighting Power

Exterior Lighting Applications	Power Limits
Building entrance (with canopy)	13 W/m^2 (1.3 W/ft^2) of canopied area
Building entrance (without canopy)	90 W/lin m (30 W/lin f) of door width
Building exit	60 W/lin m (20 W/lin f) of door width
Building facades	2 W/m^2 (0.2 W/ft^2) of vertical facade area

Exceptions to 7.4: Lighting used for the following exterior applications is exempt when equipped with an independent control device:

a. Specialized signal, directional, and marker lighting associated with transportation;
b. Lighting used to highlight features of public monuments and registered historic landmark structures or buildings;

c. Lighting that is integral to advertising signage; or

d. Lighting that is specifically designated as required by a health or life safety statute, ordinance, or regulation.

4.4 Different Shading Techniques

There are various options for shading, given below in order of effectiveness:

i. trees and shrubs

ii. trellises

iii. overhangs

iv. awnings

v. shade screens

vi. window coating and

vii. interior shades

A few descriptions about all methods of shadings are giving bellow:

i. Trees and Shrubs: Tree shading is a technique as old as mankind, but it has not been used much in modern times to reduce the mechanical cooling load. Trees offer excellent natural cooling. They throw shade over the walls and roof. Trees provide cooling bonus. To keep themselves cool, trees pump water from the ground into their leaves. As this water evaporates from the surface of the levels, it cools the trees. This 'evaporative cooling' cools the surrounding area too.

Shrubs offers less shading, but they have several other advantages. They usually cost less, reach mature size more quickly and require less space. Shrubs can shade walls and windows without blocking roof mounted solar panels.

ii. Trellises: Trellises are permanent structures that partially shade the outside of a building. Clinging vines growing over the trellises add more shade and evaporative cooling. A special trellises to shade air conditioners, heat pumps and evaporative coolers improves the equipment's performance.

Fast growing vines create shade more quickly, while trees can take years to provide useful shade. Deciduous vines, such as grape and wisteria lose their leaves in winter allowing the sun's heat to strike the building. Trellises and climbing plants are a design solution that's attractive and flexible.

iii. Shade Screens: Outside shade screens prevent sun from a window. Put these only on windows exposed to a direct sunlight. These devices are often called "sun screens" "shade clothes" or "solar shields". Unlike insect screens, shade screens are specially maid to block a certain amount of the sun's energy and emdash, usually between 50 to 90 percent of the energy striking to the outside of the window.

iv. **Awnings:** Awnings work like the visors on the baseball caps by blocking high angle sunlight. On buildings, awnings can cover individual windows or section of outside walls. They are most effective on the south side of the building.

Awnings come in a variety of shapes, sizes and colours to match many building designs. Some awnings stay in a fixed potions. Others can be rolled up in the winter to allow low angle sun to reach the building. No matter how they work, awnings are an easy way to add shading to an existing buildings. Awnings have the disadvantage of blocking the view from top half of the window.

v. **Overhangs:** Most homes have a built in shading device. Overhangs block the high angle, summer sun, but allow the lower winter sun to strike the building. As shading devices, overhangs have several limitations. For example, a roof overhang on a two story house will not shade a first story window. Nor will overhangs provide relief for east and west windows. Fixed overhangs will always be a compromise, since the sun's angle is the same in spring and autumn. You might want solar gain in March, but not in September.

vi. **Window Coatings:** Most window manufactures offer optional heat reflecting coatings that block heat gain, but allow penetration of natural light. Window that receive large amount of direct or reflected sunlight are good candidates for window coatings. This is a great choice for west-facing view windows.

vii. **Interior Shades:** Interior window shades, such as roller shades, blinds and drapes can reduce heat gain. However, interior shades don't block sunlight as well as exterior shades. Interior shades work in three ways. They reflect sunlight back out the window before it can turn into heat. They block the movement of hot air from the area around the window into the room. They insulate the room from the hot surfaces of the window glass and frame.

4.5 Different Insulating Materials

Once the house is shaded, the next major requirement is insulation. What happens is that insulation increases the house resistance to outside heat, so it takes longer for heat to get in. But the time heat does reach your living area, it is later in the day and the temperature outside is beginning to drop. Those materials that do the best job of retaining heat in the winter and keeping heat out in summer are as follows:

4.5.1 Blankets

Blankets come in rolls, usually from 16 to 24 inches wide, and are unwounded and cut to fit in place between wall studs or ceiling and floor joists.

4.5.2 Batts

Batts are similar in size to blankets but are precut to specified lengths.

4.5.3 Boards

Boards are precut to standard sizes and are usually applied with a mastic as perimeter insulation around the foundation or over existing walls for renovation work.

4.5.4 Loose-Fill

This type of insulation comes as a loose granular material in bags and can be poured into place between joists or behind walls.

4.5.5 Blown Insulation

This is a spray foam type of insulation, which is installed under pressure behind walls and between joists in ceilings and floors by professionals.

Now let's look at the qualities that the various commercial insulators have:

4.5.6 Fiberglass

Fiberglass is perhaps the most common of all insulators today; it is available in rolls or batts. The resistance of fiberglass is about 3.5 per inch of thickness. Its fire and vermin proof, moderate in cost, and easy to install. However, over some years it will tend to meet down or settle on itself. The result is that the material is compresses a bit and loses some of its insulation value.

4.5.7 Rock Wool

Rock wool is much like fiberglass, except that the material is maid from melted rock instead of glass. The resistance value is a bit less than fiberglass about 3 per inch and the problems with matting are even worse.

4.5.8 Insulating Sheathings

This is a material made from wood fibers and is usually applied on exterior walls as a backing of siding. It comes in various thicknesses, usually between ½ and 1 inch. The resistance is about 2 per inch of thickness; and though its water repellent, extended exposure to moisture will case damage through mildew and rot.

4.5.9 Plastic Insulation

The most common type of plastic insulation is polystyrene, which comes either as a blue "closed cell" foam or as white granule boards where the granules have been heat and pressure treated so that they adhere together. The resistance of these materials is about 5.5 for the blue closed cell type and 4 for the white granule type. Polyurethane on the other hand, comes as closed cell foam, boards or can be professionally blown into place inside walls, ceilings or floors as foam. In either case, its resistance value is about 6.5 per inch. Polystyrene and polyurethane tend to be expensive. Moreover, while both are good insulators and do into attract moisture or vermin, there are extreme fire hazards involved. Both will burn very rapidly and give off toxic gases, particularly when placed in a vertical position. These materials should therefore never be installed where they will be exposed. The best applications for parameter insulation on the outside of foundation walls.

4.5.10 Loose Insulators (Granule Mineral-Based)

The most common of these insulators are vermiculite and perlite, available as loose fill insulation at moderate costs. The resistance is about 2.5 per inch. These materials are fire proof and will not deteriorate from moisture, rot or insect problems. However, settling out can be a problem, particularly when they are placed in a vertical position between wall studs.

Building insulation materials are thermal insulation used in the construction or retrofit of buildings. The materials are used to reduce heat transfer by conduction, radiation or convection and are employed in varying combinations to achieve the desired outcome (usually thermal comfort with reduced energy consumption).

Insulation may be categorized by its composition (material), by its form (structural or non-structural), or by its functional mode (conductive, radioactive, convective). Non-structural forms include bats, blankets, loose-fill, spray foam, and panels. Structural forms include insulating concrete forms, structured panels, and straw bales. Sometimes a thermally reflective surface called a radiant barrier is added to a material to reduce the transfer of heat through radiation as well as conduction. Following is a table of materials, most of which has been used for insulating buildings.

R-values per inch given in SI and Imperial units (Typical values are approximations, based on the average of available results. Ranges are marked with Clicking on SI column sorts by medium value of range, click on Imperial column by lowest value

Table:4.5: R-Values for Different Materials

Materials	K	R
Vacuum insulated panel	5.28–8.8	R-30–R-50
Silica aero gel	1.76	R-10
Polyurethane rigid panel (CFC/HCFC expanded) initial	1.23–1.41	R-7–R-8
Polyurethane rigid panel (CFC/HCFC expanded) aged 5–10 years	1.10	R-6.25
Polyurethane rigid panel (pentane expanded) initial	1.20	R-6.8
Polyurethane rigid panel (pentane expanded) aged 5–10 years	0.97	R-5.5
Foil-faced polyisocyanurate rigid panel (pentane expanded) initial	1.20	R-6.8
Foil-faced polyisocyanurate rigid panel (pentane expanded) aged 5–10 years	0.97	R-5.5
Polyisocyanurate spray foam	0.76–1.46	R-4.3–R-8.3
Closed-cell polyurethane spray foam	0.97–1.14	R-5.5–R-6.5

Phenol spray foam	0.85–1.23	R-4.8–R-7
Thins late clothing insulation	1.01	R-5.75
Urea-formaldehyde panels	0.88–1.06	R-5–R-6
Urea foam	0.92	R-5.25
Extruded expanded polystyrene (XPS) high-density	0.88–0.95	R-5–R-5.4
Polystyrene board	0.88	R-5.00
Phenol rigid panel	0.70–0.88	R-4–R-5
Urea-formaldehyde foam	0.70–0.81	R-4–R-4.6
High-density fiberglass bats	0.63–0.88	R-3.6–R-5
Extruded expanded polystyrene (XPS) low-density	0.63–0.82	R-3.6–R-4.7
Cymene loose-fill (pour fill)	0.70	R-4
Molded expanded polystyrene (EPS) high-density	0.70	R-4.2
Air-entrained concrete	0.69	R-3.90
Home Foam	0.69	R-3.9
Fiberglass bats	0.55–0.76	R-3.1–R-4.3
Cotton bats (Blue Jean insulation)	0.65	R-3.7
Molded expanded polystyrene (EPS) low-density	0.65	R-3.85
Icynene spray	0.63	R-3.6
Open-cell polyurethane spray foam	0.63	R-3.6
Cardboard	0.52–0.7	R-3–R-4
Rock and slag wool bats	0.52–0.68	R-3–R-3.85
Cellulose loose-fill	0.52–0.67	R-3–R-3.8
Cellulose wet-spray	0.52–0.67	R-3–R-3.8
Rock and slag wool loose-fill	0.44–0.65	R-2.5–R-3.7
Fiberglass loose-fill	0.44–0.65	R-2.5–R-3.7
Polyethylene foam	0.52	R-3
Cementations' foam	0.35–0.69	R-2–R-3.9
Prelate loose-fill	0.48	R-2.7
Wood panels, such as sheathing	0.44	R-2.5

Fiberglass rigid panel	0.44	R-2.5
Vermiculite loose-fill	0.38–0.42	R-2.13–R-2.4
Vermiculite	0.38	R-2.13
Straw bale	0.26	R-1.45
Softwood (most)	0.25	R-1.41
Wood chips and other loose-fill wood products	0.18	R-1
Snow	0.18	R-1
Hardwood (most)	0.12	R-0.71
Brick	0.030	R-0.2
Glass	0.025	R-0.14
Poured concrete	0.014	R-0.08

4.5.11 Consideration of Materials Used

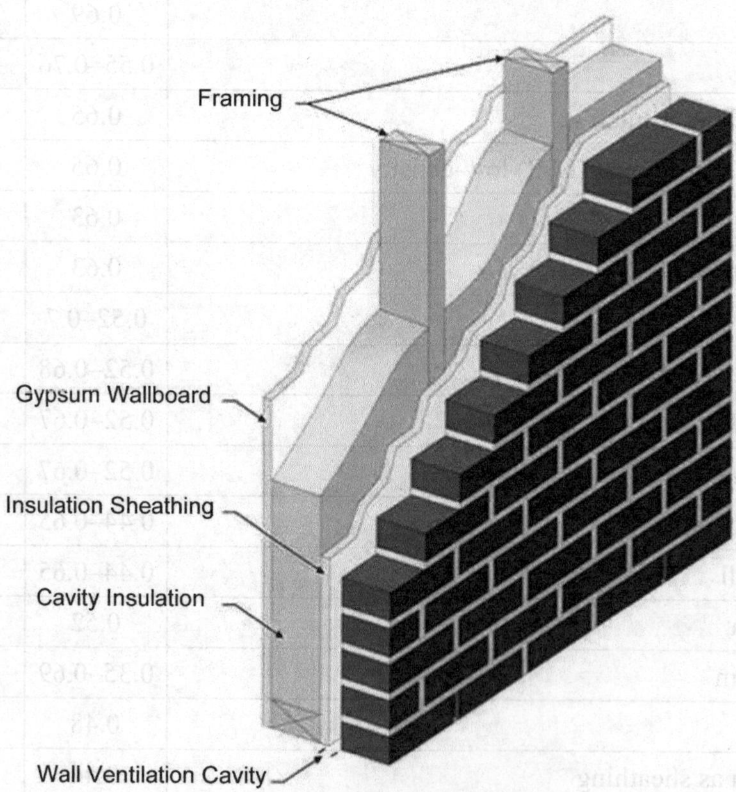

Fig.4.2: Composite Material Wall

Factors affecting the type and amount of insulation to use in a building include:

- Climate
- Ease of installation
- Durability - resistance to degradation from compression, moisture, decomposition, etc.
- Ease of replacement at end of life
- Cost effectiveness
- Toxicity
- Flammability
- Environmental impact and sustainability

Often a combination of materials is used to achieve an optimum solution and there are products which combine different types of insulation into a single form.

4.5.12 Thermal conductivity

Thermal conductivity is the quantity of heat transmitted through a unit thickness in a direction normal to a surface of unit area, due to the unit temperature gradient under steady state condition.

Table 4.7: Thermal conductivity of materials

Thermal Conductivity - k - (W/mK)			
Material/Substance	Temperature (ºC)		
	25	125	225
Acetone	0.16		
Acrylic	0.2		
Air	0.024		
Alcohol	0.17		
Aluminum	250	255	250
Aluminum Oxide	30		
Ammonia	0.022		
Antimony	18.5		
Argon	0.016		
Asbestos-cement board	0.744		
Asbestos-cement sheets	0.166		
Asbestos-cement	2.07		

Asbestos, loosely packed	0.15		
Asbestos mill board	0.14		
Asphalt	0.75		
Balsa	0.048		
Bitumen	0.17		
Benzene	0.16		
Beryllium	218		
Brass	109		
Brick dense	1.31		
Brick work	0.69		
Cadmium	92		
Carbon	1.7		
Carbon dioxide	0.0146		
Cement, Portland	0.29		
Cement, mortar	1.73		
Chalk	0.09		
Chrome Nickel Steel (18% Cr, 8 % Ni)	16.3		
Clay, dry to moist	0.15 - 1.8		
Clay, saturated	0.6 - 2.5		
Cobalt	69		
Concrete, light	0.42		
Concrete, stone	1.7		
Constantan	22		
Copper	401	400	398
Corian (ceramic filled)	1.06		
Corkboard	0.043		
Cork, regranulated	0.044		
Cork	0.07		

Cotton	0.03		
Carbon Steel	54	51	47
Cotton Wool insulation	0.029		
Diatomaceous earth (Sil-o-cel)	0.06		
Earth, dry	1.5		
Ether	0.14		
Epoxy	0.35		
Felt insulation	0.04		
Fiberglass	0.04		
Fiber insulating board	0.048		
Fiber hardboard	0.2		
Fireclay brick 500°C	1.4		
Foam glass	0.045		
Freon 12	0.073		
Gasoline	0.15		
Glass	1.05		
Glass, Pearls, dry	0.18		
Glass, Pearls, saturated	0.76		
Glass, window	0.96		
Glass, wool Insulation	0.04		
Glycerol	0.28		
Gold	310	312	310
Granite	1.7 - 4.0		
Gypsum or plaster board	0.17		
Hair felt	0.05		
Hardboard high density	0.15		
Hardwoods (oak, maple...)	0.16		
Helium	0.142		

Hydrogen	0.168		
Ice (0°C, 32°F)	2.18		
Insulation materials	0.035 - 0.16		
Iridium	147		
Iron	80	68	60
Iron, wrought	59		
Iron, cast	55		
Kapok insulation	0.034		
Kerosene	0.15		
Lead Pb	35		
Leather, dry	0.14		
Limestone	1.26 - 1.33		
Magnesia insulation (85%)	0.07		
Magnetite	4.15		
Magnesium	156		
Marble	2.08 - 2.94		
Mercury	8		
Methane	0.030		
Methanol	0.21		
Mica	0.71		
Mineral insulation materials, wool blankets...	0.04		
Molybdenum	138		
Monel	26		
Nickel	91		
Nitrogen	0.024		
Nylon 6	0.25		
Oil, machine lubricating SAE 50	0.15		

Olive oil	0.17		
Oxygen	0.024		
Paper	0.05		
Paraffin Wax	0.25		
Perlite, atmospheric pressure	0.031		
Perlite, vacuum	0.00137		
Plaster, gypsum	0.48		
Plaster, metal lath	0.47		
Plaster, wood lath	0.28		
Plastics, foamed (insulation materials)	0.03		
Plastics, solid			
Platinum	70	71	72
Plywood	0.13		
Polyethylene HD	0.42 - 0.51		
Polypropylene	0.1 - 0.22		
Polystyrene expanded	0.03		
Polyurethane	0.02		
Porcelain	1.5		
PTFE	0.25		
PVC	0.19		
Pyrex glass	1.005		
Quartz mineral	3		
Rock, solid	2 - 7		
Rock, porous volcanic (Tuff)	0.5 - 2.5		
Rock Wool insulation	0.045		
Sand, dry	0.15 - 0.25		
Sand, moist	0.25 - 2		

Sand, saturated	2 - 4		
Sandstone	1.7		
Sawdust	0.08		
Silica aero gel	0.02		
Silicone oil	0.1		
Silver	429		
Snow (temp < 0°C)	0.05 - 0.25		
Sodium	84		
Softwoods (fir, pine ...)	0.12		
Soil, with organic matter	0.15 - 2		
Soil, saturated	0.6 - 4		
Steel, Carbon 1%	43		
Stainless Steel	16	17	19
Straw insulation	0.09		
Styrofoam	0.033		
Tin Sn	67		
Zinc Zn	116		
Urethane foam	0.021		
Vermiculite	0.058		
Vinyl ester	0.25		
Water	0.58		
Water, vapor (steam)		0.016	
Wood across the grain, white pine	0.12		
Wood across the grain, balsa	0.055		
Wood across the grain, yellow pine	0.147		
Wood, oak	0.17		
Wool, felt	0.07		

1W/ (mK) =1W/ (m degree C) = 0.85984 kcal / (h m degree C) = 0.5779Btu/ft h degree F)

4.6 ENERGY CONSERVATION DESIGN GUIDELINES

4.6.1 Buildings

- Specify caulking and weather-stripping on all windows, doors, utility penetrations, Building cracks and crevices.
- Evaluate the use of double glazing and reflective coatings on windows.
- Evaluate the use of reflective coatings on flat roofs.
- Use minimum ceiling heights to minimize volume of area to be environmentally Controlled
- Optimize the ratio of roof and wall area to interior volume to reduce the exterior Surface area available.
- Locate corridors, stairwells, elevator shafts, storage rooms, etc. on exterior to act as a buffer between exterior and conditioned space-west exposure when air-conditioning is significant, north exposure when heating is significant.
- Utilize natural lighting when cost of electrical energy saved will exceed cost of Additional energy required for air conditioning and heating.

Table:4.8: RSI & R values of different insulating materials

S.No.	Insulation Materials		Thickness		Thermal Resistance	
			mm	inch	RSI m^2*°C/W	R ft^2*h*°F/ BTU
1.	Flexible (mineral wool, glass fiber)	low density	140	5-1/2	2.83	16
		medium density	140	5-1/2	3.30	19
		high density	140	5-1/2	3.93	22.5
2.	Loose fill	glass fiber	100	4	2.00	11
		mineral fiber	100	4	2.30	13
		cellulose fiber	100	4	2.50	12.5
3.	Spray	polyurethane	100	4	4.1	23
		isocyanurate	100	4	3.4	19
		cellulose fiber	100	4	2.4	13.5

4.6.2 Building Architecture

a. Minimize wall and glass area exposed to the south, southwest, and west when air conditioning vice heating is expected to be the major load. Architectural shading, tinted glass or solar screening should be considered for all glass having these exposures. For applications where heating is the major concern, more glass exposure to the south, southwest, and west and less to the north would be desirable. Shading would not be required.

b. Locate parking areas to avoid creating heat islands adjacent to the building.

4.6.3 Insulation - save money and energy

As far as keeping warm is concerned, insulation is the first thing to consider. A huge amount of heat is lost through loft spaces and walls. But it doesn't have to be this way. There is a lot that can be done to reduce heat loss, including some measures, such as draught-proofing, which do not cost much money and do not need skilled installers. Further information can be obtained from the Energy Saving Trust and the National Energy Foundation. The Renewable Energy Centre website contains information on home energy saving with links to suppliers and contractors.

4.7 Different Ventilation Techniques

The next step is to get these cool breezes into and through the house. Let's look at how to maximize the cooling effect with ventilation and where we want the air to flow. The factors involved with natural ventilation cooling are s follows:

i. The summer prevailing wind velocity and direction
ii. The location from where we take air into the house
iii. The location from which air exits
iv. The time of day and
v. The outside air temperature and humidity

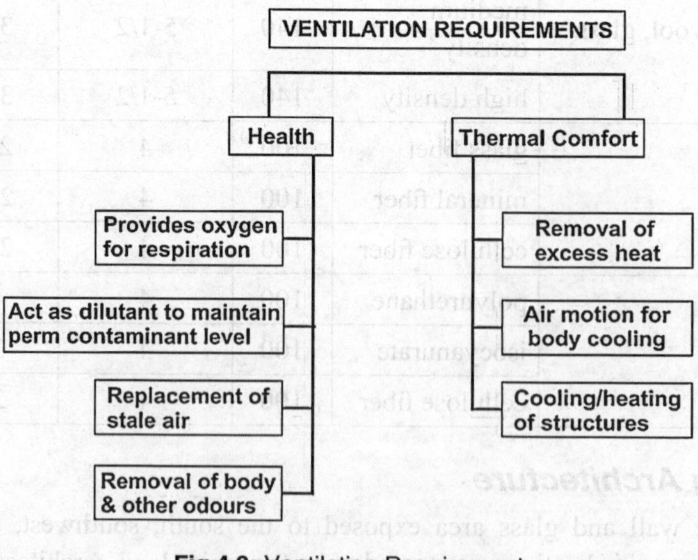

Fig.4.3: Ventilation Requirement

The insulation of high and low air vents is one effective method of achieving summer ventilation. The hot air in your house will rise and exit from the high vent while the cool air will be drawn in through the low vent. The location of vents is important. You should try to have your intake vent on the windward side of the house and your outlet vent on the leeward side. In many instances the direction of the prevailing winds will vary during the day and night. If this applied to your site, plan to locate most of your inlet vents on the evening side to achieve the maximum evening airflow, as the major cooling of your house will occur at this time. These vent must also be operable so they can be sealed during the winter months and on hot sunny days.

Another consideration when placing vents is to minimize any impediment to the flow of air to the vents, such as shade trees or wind breaks. In the case of shade trees, the air will move freely to the vent as long as the crown of the tree is not in direct line with it. Make sure that the crowns of shade trees are above these vents or else install the vents on either side of the crowns. If there are conflicts with windbreaks because winter winds and summer breezes come from the same direction, you will have to balance these effects. Generally, the summer ventilation needs will be most important, as you can eliminate the windbreak and still minimize winter air infiltration by using the other techniques as discussed bellow:

If a private outdoor patio area is desired and the windbreak then serves to enclose this area, use vents along the wall area outside the protected patio area for ventilation. Other important factors involved in achieving efficient airflow through a house are, first the location of interior walls and, second the size of operable windows and vents. This is because the speed of air flow depends on the size and position of the of the inlet and exhaust openings (doors, windows, vents etc.) and the speed of the external cooling breezes. Natural cooling will occur when the cool air will allowed to enter a house and replace warm air. Hence, by increasing the velocity of air passing through a structure, you increase the cooling effect.

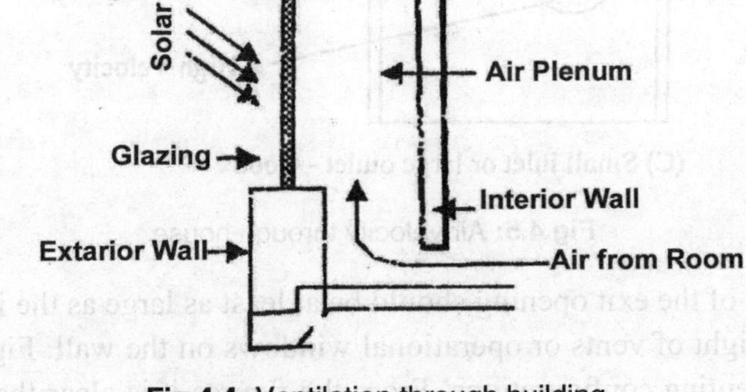

Fig.4.4: Ventilation through building

Since air velocity through the house is needed for cooling, Fig. 4.4 shows the effect of relative inlet and outlet vent sizes. Normally, maximum flow is desired, and if outside humidity is high, the most cooling will take place by increased internal airflow velocity. This is done by decreasing the inlet opening and leaving the large exit opening.

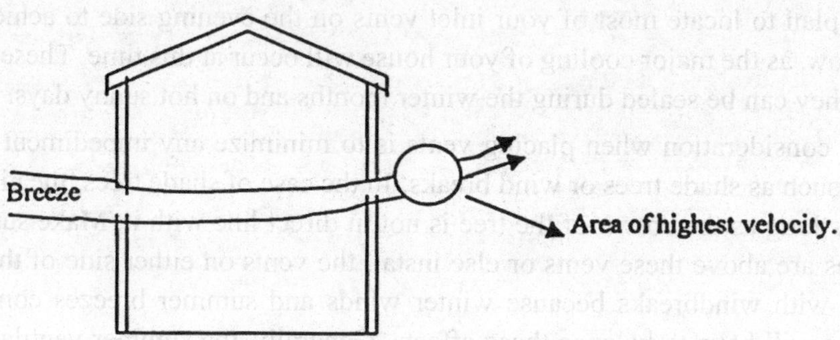

(A) Large inlet / small outlet - poor

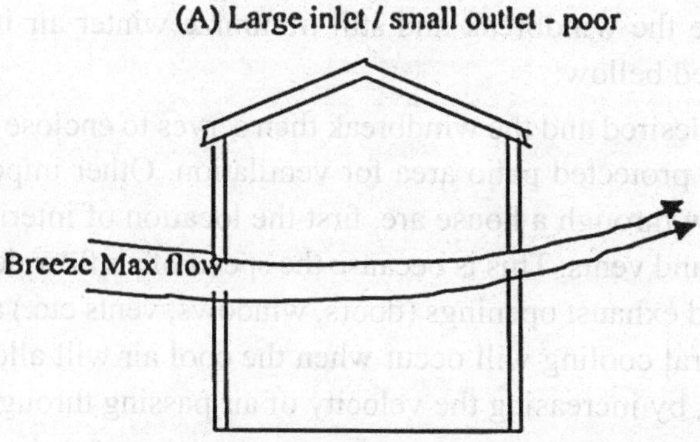

(B) Inlet = Outlet area - Fair

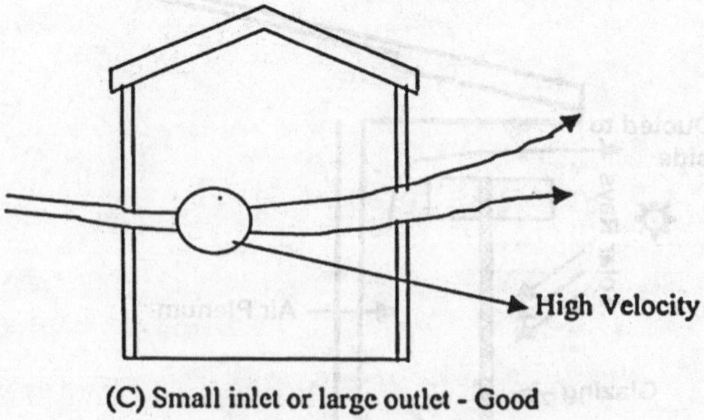

(C) Small inlet or large outlet - Good

Fig.4.5: Air velocity through house

Therefore the area of the exit opening should be at least as large as the inlet opening. The final consideration is the height of vents or operational windows on the wall. Figure 4.5(a) to (c) show the effect of various venting configurations. From the figures it is clear that while the size of the outlet is important, its positions on the wall is somewhat arbitrary inlet vents. To decide which arrangement is best for you, first decide what area you want to ventilation for example, if you want to vent the ceiling area, use the shows in Fig. 4.5(a); if you want to vent the floor area, use the arrangement shown in fig 4.5(c). As you can see there are several choices. Generally, Fig. 4.5(c) works best since you benefit from the temperature differences (e.g. chimney effect) was well as from the wind movement, and using high wall outlet vents and ceiling and attic vents can increase the chimney effect even more.

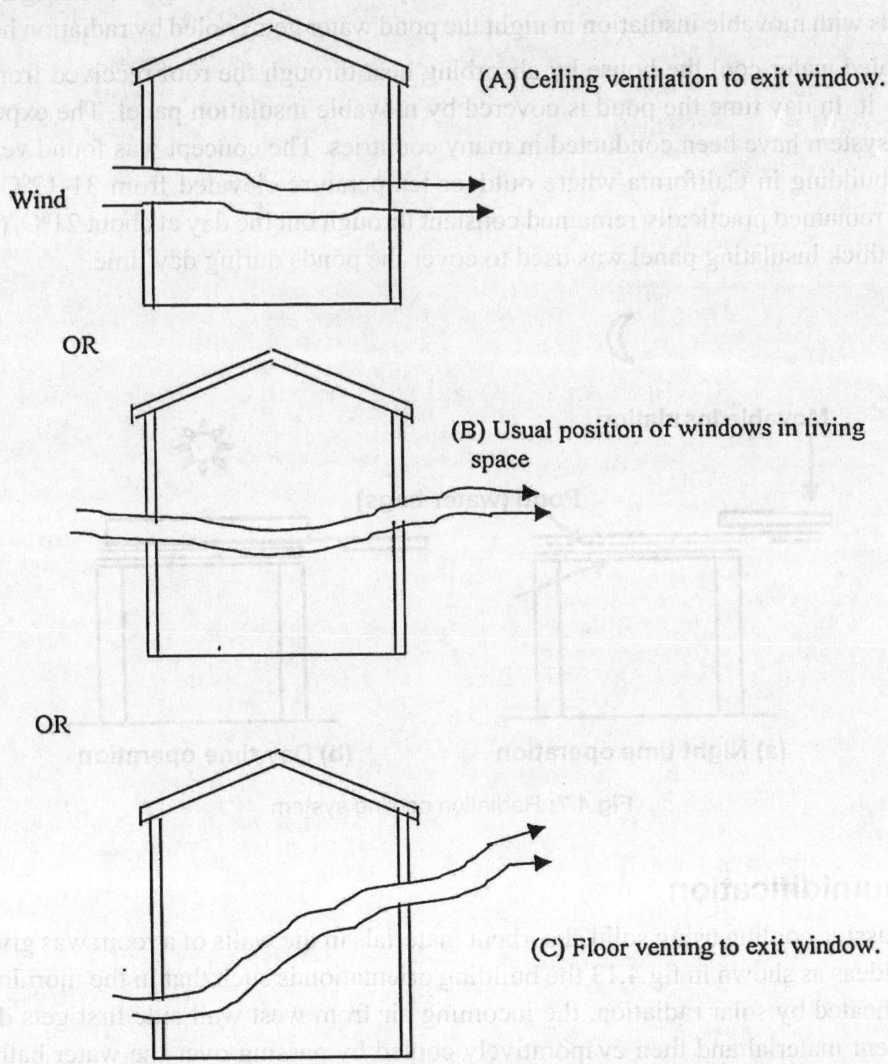

Fig.4.6: Any part of the room can be vented by adjusting the position of the inlet

The decision to use a fan will be determined by your local conditions. Generally humid southern regions of the country require a high volume of air velocity passing over the body. In regions with low humidity, on the other hand, cooling will take place by evaporation of the moisture from the skin, so a lower air volume will produce a comfortable cooling effect.

4.8 Radiation Cooling

Radiation cooling occur when a building at higher temperature radiates energy to sky at lower temperature. During the night sky is an ideal heat sink for radiate cooling. The amount of radiation cooling between building and sky depends on many parameters like the temperature of the building its surface remittance and orientation. There are many methods of cooling of building by radiation, such as ponds with movable insulation in night the pond water gets cooled by radiation heat transfer.

The cooled water cool the house by absorbing heat through the roof received from space the space below it. In day time the pond is covered by movable insulation panel. The experiments on this type of system have been conducted in many countries. The concept was found very effective in full size building in California where outdoor temperature elevated from 31-12°C. The room temperature remained practically remained constant through out the day at about 21°C, (Table 4.12) when 15cm thick insulating panel was used to cover the ponds during day time.

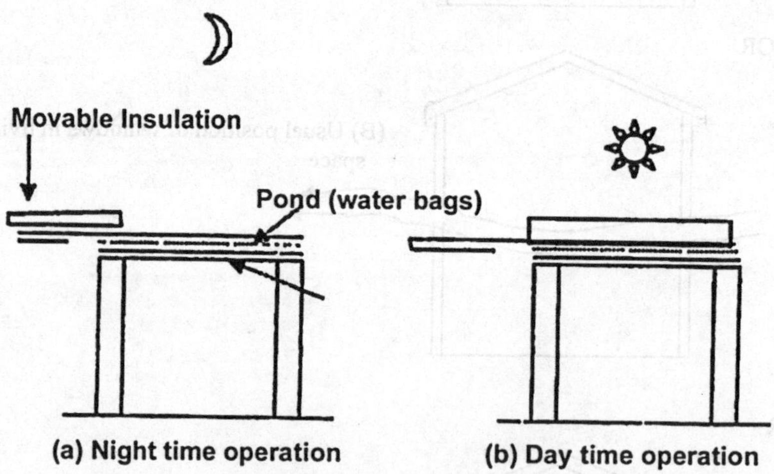

Fig.4.7: Radiation cooling system

4.9 Dehumidification

An idea of passive cooling using solid absorbent materials in the walls of a room was given by Alter rich. In this ideas as shown in fig 4.13 the building orientation is such that in the morning when the cast wall is heated by solar radiation, the incoming air from west wall side first gets dried by the solid absorbent material and then evaporatively cooled by passing over the water baths and flow into the room. The hot air going out of the room regenerates the solid absorbent material on the east wall side. In the evening the west wall is heated by the sun, the reversal of the air flow occurs. The system appears to be alterative but depends on solar radiation and relative humidity and also puts a restriction on the building design.

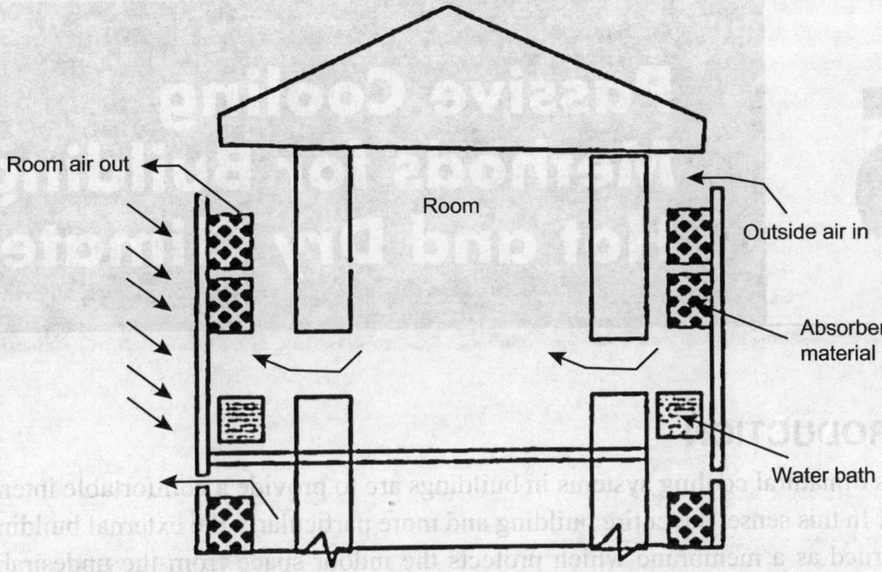

Fig.4.8: A house cooled by dehumidification and evaporative cooling

5 Passive Cooling Methods for Building in Hot and Dry Climate

5.1 INTRODUCTION

The purposes of natural cooling systems in buildings are to provide a comfortable internal thermal environment. In this sense, the entire building and more particularly the external building envelope can be construed as a membrane which protects the indoor space from the undesirable climatic influence. At its best the external envelope will not only filter out the worst external elements passively but also interact positively with the outdoor environment to remove even the internally generated heat. It will thus combine the effects of both insulation and mechanical cooling.

5.2 INTERNAL THERMAL ENVIRONMENT

The internal thermal environment of a naturally cooled building results from the response of the building to the changing external climatic influences which repeat themselves in daily and annual cycles. The relative importance of the daily cycle (which has a frequency of 24 hours) and that of the annual cycle (frequency 365 days) depends upon the geographical location of site under consideration. Near the poles, the annual cycle is of greatest importance while at the equator, the daily cycle plays a major role in determining the quality of shelter needed.

From the building designers point of view, the important climate elements are (i) solar radiation (its intensity and direction and duration of sunshine hours) (ii) air temperature (iii) humidity and precipitation (iv) wind (speed and direction) and (v) clearness of the sky or atmosphere.

5.2.1 Solar Radiation

The direction of solar radiation depends upon the latitude of the place and the declination of the sun on the day in question while the intensity of radiation depends upon the clearness of the atmosphere (the absence of dust particles, water vapour, etc.). The intensity of solar radiation is nearly constant outside the earth's atmosphere but as the radiation travels through the atmosphere to the ground, its intensity is reduced, and its direction and spectral distribution changed due to absorption, scattering and reflection by carbon-di-oxide, ozone, water vapour and dust particles present in the atmosphere. Clouds reflect back a part of solar radiation also.

The potential intensity of solar radiation depends upon the length of the earth's atmosphere through which the rays must travel and therefore at low solar altitudes, the intensity is less than at high solar altitudes (Fig. 5.1). The effect of solar radiation on buildings is to cause heating of the exposed building surfaces and of building interior because of radiation coming in through windows.

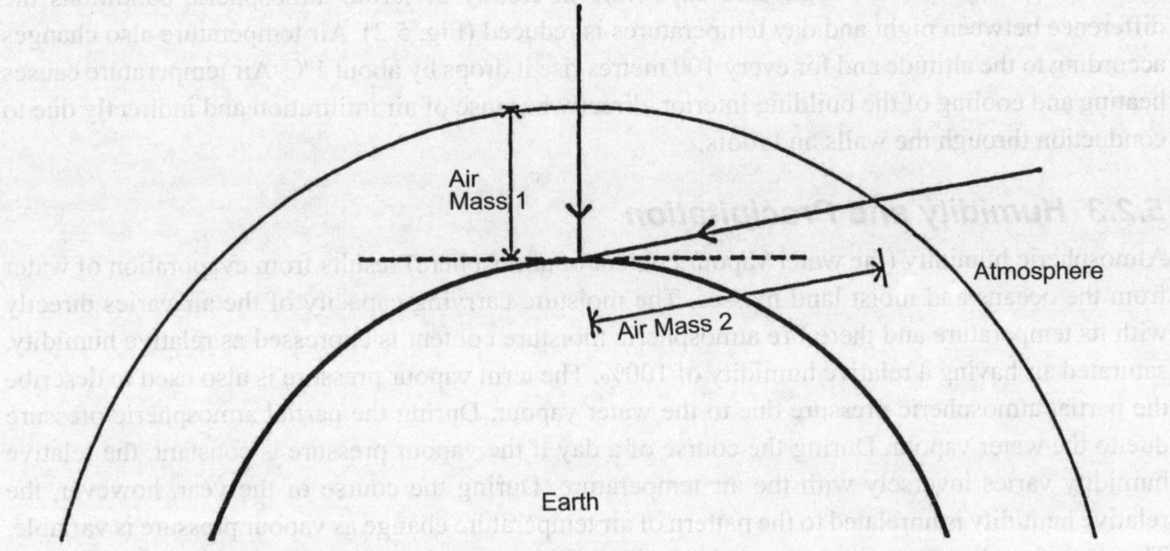

Fig.5.1: Reduction in solar intensity due to air mass and solar altitude

5.2.2 Ambient Air Temperature

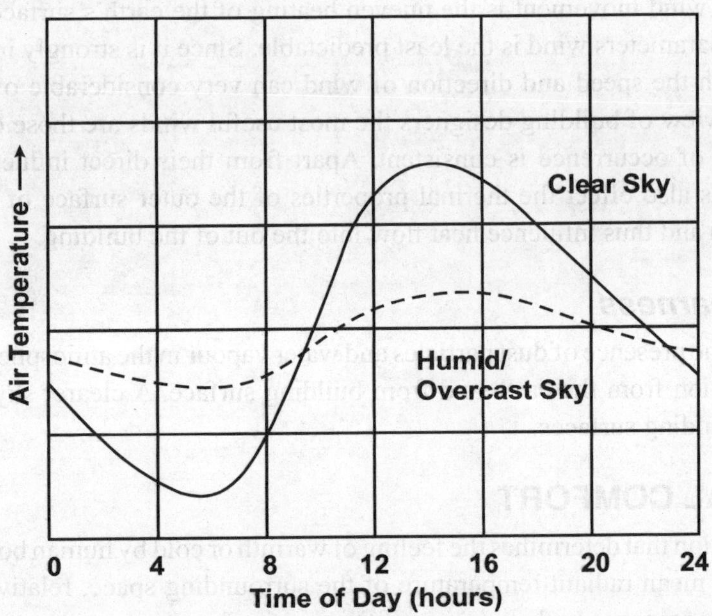

Fig.5.2: Diurnal temperature variation in a humid climate, desert climate

The ambit air temperature mainly depends upon the heating of the earth's surface by solar radiation and its cooling by outgoing radiation. Air temperature is minimum just before sunrise and it reaches its maximum value sometime in the afternoon. Under clear sky conditions the air temperature fluctuates greatly between night and day while in cloudy or turbid atmospheric conditions the difference between night and day temperatures is reduced (Fig. 5.2). Air temperature also changes according to the altitude and for every 100 metres rise it drops by about 1^{0}C. Air temperature causes heating and cooling of the building interior, directly because of air infiltration and indirectly due to conduction through the walls and roofs.

5.2.3 Humidity and Precipitation

Atmospheric humidity (the water vapour content of atmosphere) results from evaporation of water from the oceans and moist land masses. The moisture carrying capacity of the air varies directly with its temperature and therefore atmospheric moisture content is expressed as relative humidity, saturated air having a relative humidity of 100%. The term vapour pressure is also used to describe the partial atmospheric pressure due to the water vapour. During the partial atmospheric pressure due to the water vapour. During the course of a day if the vapour pressure is constant, the relative humidity varies inversely with the air temperature. During the course of the year, however, the relative humidity is unrelated to the pattern of air temperature change as vapour pressure is variable. The over abundance of water vapour in the atmosphere causes precipitation cause changes in the thermal properties of building elements.

5.2.4 Wind

The main cause of wind movement is the uneven heating of the earth's surface by solar radiation of all the climatic parameters wind is the least predictable. Since it is strongly influenced by terrain characteristics, both the speed and direction of wind can very considerable over short distances. From the point of view of building designers the most useful winds are those of which the speed, direction and time of occurrence is consistent. Apart from their direct influence on the internal environment, winds also effect the thermal properties of the outer surface of the building (outer surface coefficient) and thus influence heat flow into the out of the building.

5.2.5 Sky Clearness

This refers to the presence of dust particles and water vapour in the atmosphere which influences the outgoing radiation from the earth and from building surface. A clearer sky at night generally results in cooler building surfaces.

5.3 THERMAL COMFORT

The physical condition that determines the feeling of warmth or cold by human body is a combination of air temperature, mean radiant temperature of the surrounding space, relative humidity and air velocity. The human response to the same conditions varies from person to person and for the same person the response depends upon the clothing on the body and the nature of activity the person is engaged in apart from these two factors, a number of other psychological and environmental factors also influence the feeling of thermal comfort. The basic thermal balance equation given by Fanger (1973) relates three independent physiological measures skin temperature, sweet rate and metabolic rate to the four environmental parameters and to the level of clothing. This equation given the condition in which the bodily heat generated equals the heat lost and no lowering or raising of body temperature is taking place. This of course is unrelated to the level of thermal comfort experienced by an individual.

Various researchers have attempted to combine the effect of the environmental parameters into one single index of comfort (Givoni, 1969) but there is as yet no universally applicable or universally accepted index of comfort. Till recently, the most commonly used index was the "Effective Temperature" index which has been replaced by the *"Standard Effective Temperature"* (Gagge, 1972) in which any environment, clothing and activity level is expressed in terms of a uniform environment (air temperature equals mean radiant temperature) standardized at 50% relative humidity, air velocity of 0.125/m/sec/, for lightly clothed subjects in sedentary occupations. A similar index for tropical conditions called "Tropical Summer Index" for Indian conditions this is the most applicable index. Fig 5.3 shown TSI plotted on a psychrometric chart. The equation of TSI is:

$$T.S.I = 0.308\, t_w + 0.74\, t_g - 2.06\, V^{1/2} + 0.841$$

Where

t_w = wet bulb temperature

t_g = globe temperature

V = air velocity in m/sec

The equation is simplified as

$$T.S.I = 0.33\, t_w + 0.74\, t_g - 2.06\, V^{1/2}$$

for rapid determination of the comfort index. The comfortable range of T.S.I given by

Thermal sensation	Range	Optimum value
Slightly cool	19.0 – 25.0 °C	22.0 °C
Comfortable	25.0 – 30.0 °C	27.5 °C
Slightly warm	30.0 – 34.0 °C	32.0 °C

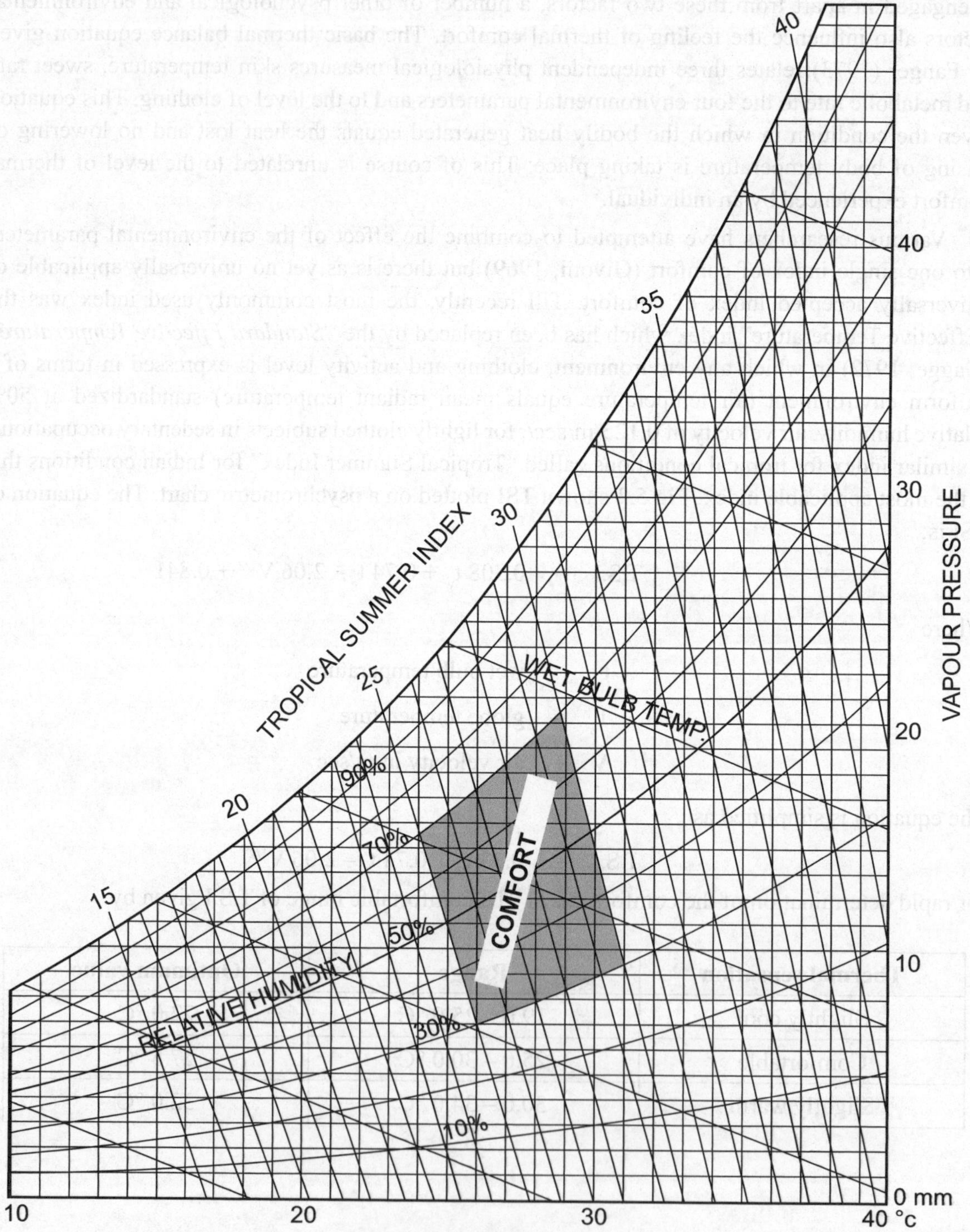

Fig.5.3: TSI on a psychrometic chart

It has been seen from equation above that the effect of increased humidity (given by t_w) is similar to that of increased air temperatures and mean radiant temperature (accounted for by t_g), while the effect of increased air velocity is to reduce the T.S.I value. The last is strictly true only within the temperature ranges given above and at higher temperatures increased velocity does not result in lowering of the comfort index (Givoni, 1967).

For summer conditions in buildings, therefore, the air temperature and mean radiant temperature need to be kept low, while relative humidity and air velocity can be controlled to relieve the effect of higher temperatures.

5.4 THERMOPHYSICAL PROPERTIES OF BUILDING ELEMENTS

The response of the building fabric to the outdoor environment depends upon certain thermophysical properties of the building elements.

The most important of these are:

i. Outer surface characteristic – Absorptivity, reflectivity and emissivity for radiation; under surface coefficient of heat transfer.
ii. Material characteristics- thermal conductivity, heat capacity, density

5.4.1 Outer Surface Characteristics

Of the total radiation incident on an opaque surface, a part is reflected and a part is absorbed. Reflectivity of the surface is that part of the total incident radiation which is reflected while absorptivity of the surface is that part of the total radiation which is absorbed. Both these properties are wave length dependent. In general it can be said that polished metallic surfaces are good reflector at all wave length while light coloured painted surfaces are good reflectors for solar radiation but not for thermal radiation. Emissivity which defines the radiation emission properties of a surface at a particular wave length is the emissive power of the surface as compared to the emissive power of a perfect radiator or black body. For a given wave length the surface emissivity equals the absorptivity. However, in practice, absorptivity is of interest only at wave lengths of solar radiation while emissivity is to be measured for far infrared wave length radiation that is emitted by terrestrial objects. For most materials these two are not same. The colour of a surface is a good indicator of absorptivity but not of emissivity which depends only upon surface structure. White wash and oxidized aluminium foil have nearly equal absorptivity (0.12 and 0.15, respectively) but their emissivity is very different (0.90 and 0.12 respectively).

The surface coefficient defines the rate of heat exchange between the surface and surrounding air, and the radiation exchange with the surrounding surfaces, or the sky. The radiative part of the surface coefficient depends upon the emissivity of the surface and upon the temperatures of the radiation exchanging surfaces. The convective part of the surface coefficient depends upon the velocity of air near the surface as well as on the texture of the surface. Vertical surfaces are usually exposed to other vertical surfaces at near equal temperatures in contrast with horizontal surfaces which are exposed to the sky. Therefore, the radiative component of vertical surface coefficient becomes very small as compared to that of horizontal surfaces and it is usually neglected in calculation.

5.4.2 Material Characteristics

The most important property of building material is its thermal conductivity (k) which determines the rate at which heat is conductivity through the material. The inverse of thermal conductivity is the resistivity which, as the name implies, is a measure of the resistance which the material offers to the passage of heat. Another important property of the building material is the volumetric heat capacity which is the quantity of heat required to raise the temperature of a unit volume of the material by 1^0C. This is given by the product of specific heat (c) and the density (r) of the material. For non air-conditioned building another property of the material called *"thermal diffusivity"* (or in more descriptive terms, *"temperature conductivity"*) is useful. This is the ratio of the heat conducted by the material to the heat stored up in it and is given by k/r.c. and is measured in m^2/deg. hour.

5.4.3 Building Element Characteristics

Building elements usually consist of more than one material. For instance, a simple brick wall usually has a plaster layer on both sides of it. A typical reinforced concrete roof has a plaster layer underneath and various water proofing layers above it. The properties of the building element are then derived from the thermophysical properties of different material layers. Three of these properties are important in the present context. The U-value of an element is its conductance for heat and it depends upon the thermal conductivity of the materials and the thickness of the different layers. For composite elements the U-value is the inverse of the sum of the resistance of the individual layers. Air to air U-values also take into account the resistance between the building elements surfaces and the surrounding air and are a useful measure of the heat conducted by the building element under steady state conditions, i.e. when the temperatures on both sides of the element remain constant.

When building elements are subjected to temperature fluctuations, not only the heat transmitted by the element but also the time taken for heat to travel through, the element becomes important. Another property of building element called 'time lag' may now be defined. A fluctuating temperature wave outside the building element, gives rise to another temperature wave with lower amplitude on the inside. The two temperature waves are out of phase by an angle called time lag which depends upon the thermal diffusivity and thickness of the building element. In Fig. 5.5 time lag is given by the difference in hours between the occurrence of the peak temperature outdoors and the corresponding peak temperature indoors. The ratio of the amplitude of internal temperature wave to the amplitude of external temperature wave is called the *"decrement factor"*. Massive building elements such as brick walls usually have a large time lag (Fig. 5.4) and lower decrement factor than thinner elements of light weight materials.

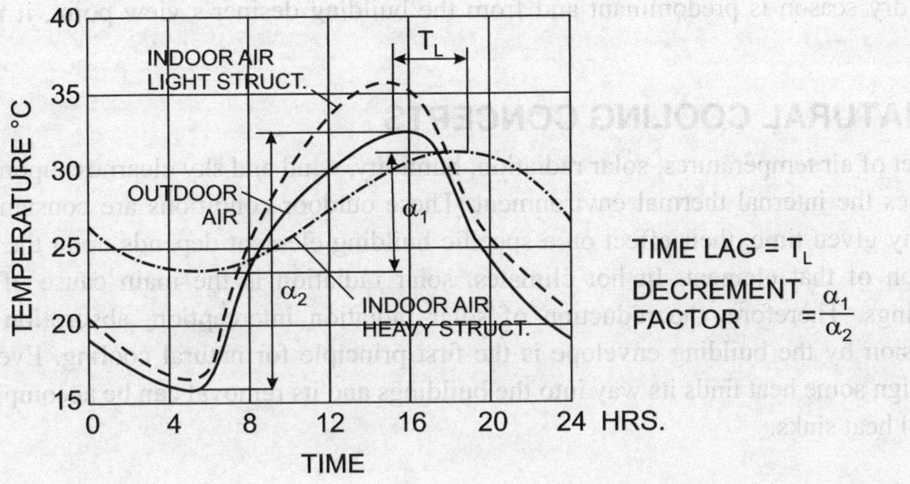

Fig.5.4: Effect of thermal capacity of building elements on time lag and decrement factor

5.5 CLIMATE

Miller (1961) has classified climates into the following types:

k. Hot climates
   i. Hot dry: hot deserts
   ii. Warm wet: equatorial and tropical marine
   iii. Hot dry and warm wet: tropical continental and monsoon

l. Warm temperature climates
   i. Western margin type
   ii. Eastern margin type

m. Cool temperature climates
   i. Cool temperature
   ii. Cool temperature marine

n. Cold climates
   i. Cold continental: Siberian
   ii. Cold marine: Norwegian
   iii. Cold desert
   iv. Arctic

Hot dry and hot dray and warm wet are the only two climate types that are found in the Northern Indian plains and are being discussed in the following pages. These two climate types are characterised by a large diurnal temperature variation, low humidity (during summer in climate type 3) clear skies, intense solar radiation, dusty winds and high air temperatures during day time.

The hot dry season is predominant and from the building desiner's view point, it is the critical season.

5.6 NATURAL COOLING CONCEPTS

The effect of air temperatures, solar radiation, humidity, wind and sky clearness upon the building determines the internal thermal environment. These outdoor conditions are constantly changing and at any given time, their effect on a specific building element depends upon the location and orientation of that element. In hot climates, solar radiation is the main cause of overheating of buildings. Therefore, the reduction of solar radiation interception, absorption and inward transmission by the building envelope is the first principle for natural cooling. Even with good solar design some heat finds its way into the buildings and its removal can be accomplished by use of natural heat sinks.

5.6.1 Solar heat gain reduction

The solar radiation intercepted by the building can be greatly reduced by choosing a proper building form and by orienting it with due regard to solar geometry. Some of the important aspects of solar control through building design are mentioned below.

The solar radiation received by a building element is dependent upon its orientation. For an isolated building with each of the four walls and the roof of equal area, the relative heat load due to direct solar radiation is given in Table. 5.1.

Table 5.1:Direct solar heat load on different building surfaces for latitudes 17° to 31°C north and south

	Roof	Walls			
		North	South	East	West
Summer (June 22)	48-51%	6-13%	0-2%	19-20%	19-20%
Winter (Dec., 21)	28-34%	0%	35-44%	14-15%	14-15%

In addition to the direct radiation, the building receives diffuse and reflected radiation also. Measured values of solar radiation (Mani, 1981) show that during the summer months in India the diffuse radiation is about one third of the total radiation and during monsoons it is more than half of the total radiation. Irrespective of their orientation walls receive equal amounts of diffuse radiation while the roof receives about twice as much.

From the foregoing it is clear that the south wall receives the least radiation in summer and the most in winter. The east and west walls receive equal amounts of radiation, more in summer than in winter. The north wall receives radiation only in summer and the roof receives a large proportion of radiation in summer and the roof receives a large proportion of radiation summer but much less in winter. The most favourable orientation is therefore due south. All building elements need to be shaded from solar radiation in summer but shading is vital for glazed areas (windows) as nearly all the solar radiation incident upon the unprotected glazed elements enters the building to be absorbed by internal surface. Structural shading devices (horizontal, vertical and inclined louvers), movable screens, deciduous trees and plants can all be used to control direct solar radiation but the effectiveness of sun shades is not equal for all orientations of walls and, therefore windows should be provided only in those positions where effective protection against the sun can be ensured. Protection against diffuse and reflected radiation cannot be provided by any simple method. Shading is easiest to provide on south wall where a horizontal projection of appropriate depth will exclude the summer sun while still permitting sunlight in the building in winter (Fig. 5.5). The east and west walls can be protected by a combination of horizontal and vertical louvers but fixed shading devices of this kind cannot be designed to allow sunlight in winter. A better method is to use movable screens on the east and west walls. The north wall can be protected easily by vertical louvers. The roof can be shaded only by a horizontal cover (a false roof) extending over the whole roof and projecting beyond it on the east and west sides. Surface shading can be provided as an integral part of the building element also. Highly textured walls have a part of their surface in shade (Fig. 5.6). The increased surface area of such a wall results in an increased outer surface coefficient, which permits the sunlight surface to stay cooler as well as to cool down faster at night.

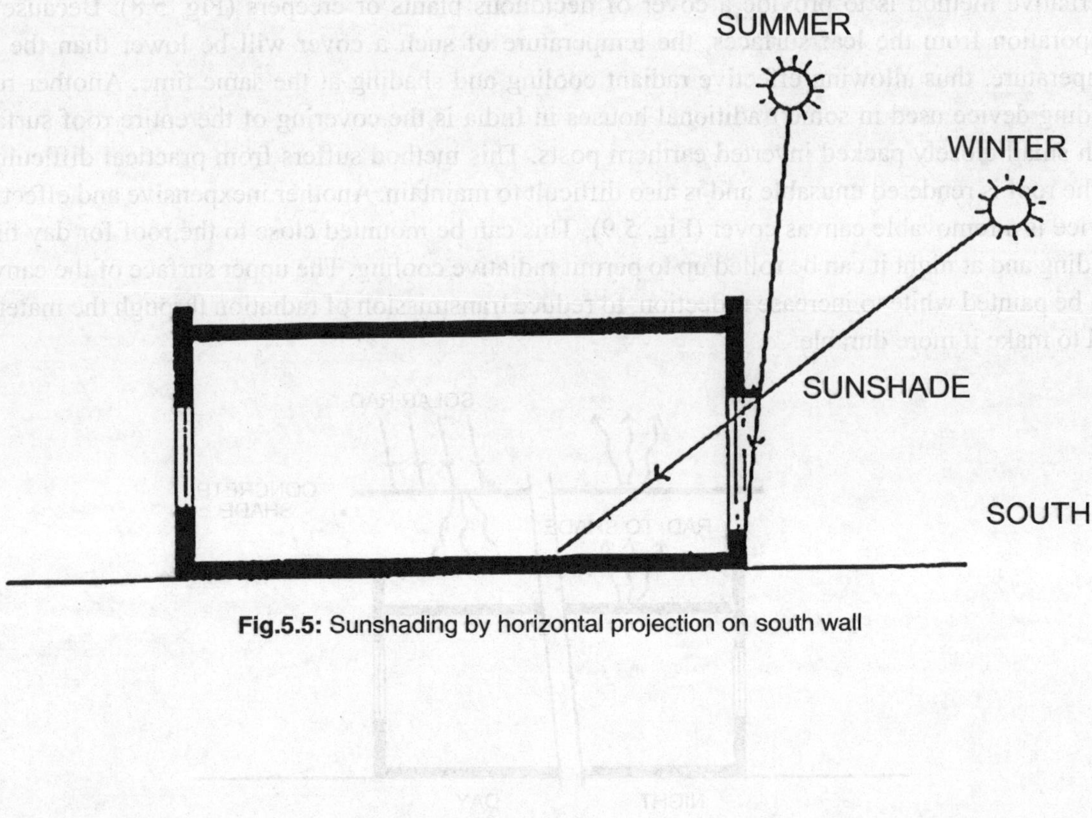

Fig.5.5: Sunshading by horizontal projection on south wall

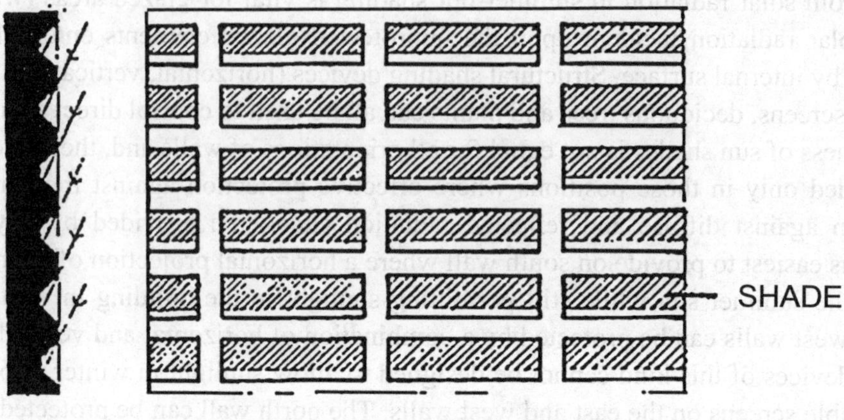

Fig.5.6: Shading due to surface texture

External shading devices used on a building surface should not interfere with night time radiative cooling. This is particularly important for roof surfaces which are exposed to the cool night sky. A solid cover of concrete or galvanised iron sheets (Fig. 5.7) will shade the roof from solar radiation but it will not permit the roof to cool down by radiation to the night sky. An alternative method is to provide a cover of deciduous plants or creepers (Fig. 5.8). Because of evaporation from the leaf surfaces, the temperature of such a cover will be lower than the air temperature, thus allowing effective radiant cooling and shading at the same time. Another roof shading device used in some traditional houses in India is the covering of the entire roof surface with small closely packed inverted earthern posts. This method suffers from practical difficulties as the roof is rendered unusable and is also difficult to maintain. Another inexpensive and effective device is a removable canvas cover (Fig. 5.9). This can be mounted close to the roof for day time shading and at night it can be rolled up to permit radiative cooling. The upper surface of the canvas can be painted white to increase reflection, to reduce transmission of radiation through the material and to make it more durable.

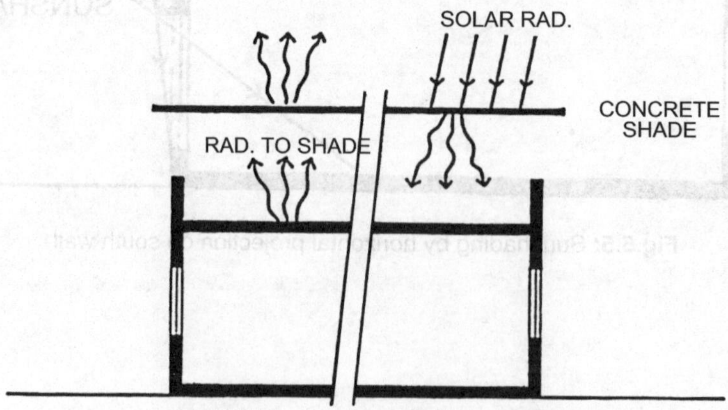

Fig.5.7: Roof shading by a solid cover

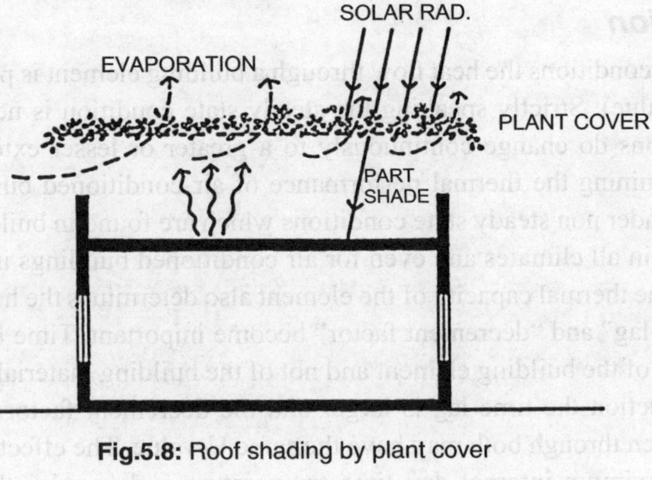

Fig.5.8: Roof shading by plant cover

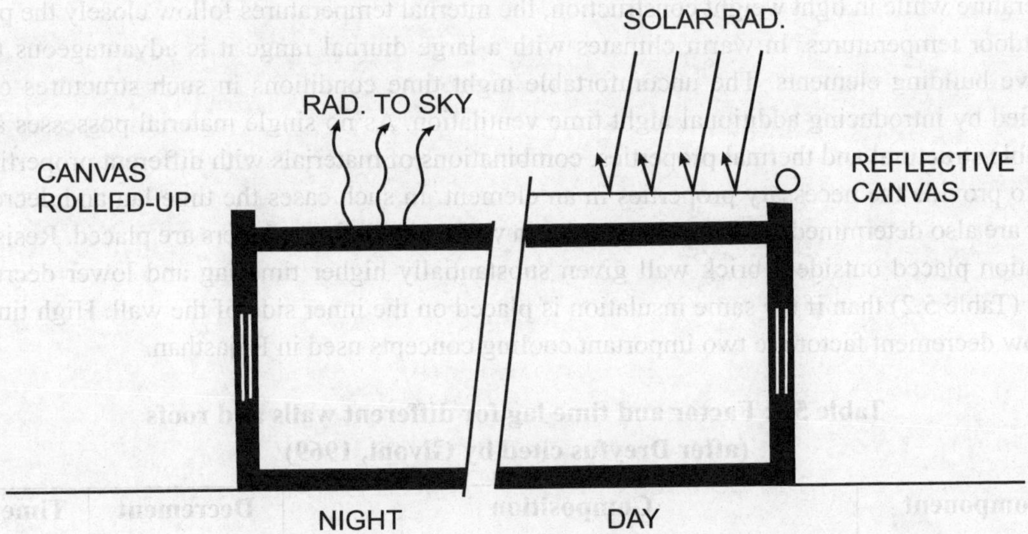

Fig.5.9: Roof shading by removable fabric cover permits radiant cooling at night

The reflection and emission properties of surfaces finishes need to be controlled to reflect away most of solar radiation and to allow cooling by radiation at night. The ideal surface finish would have very high reflectivity and emissivity. It can be seen from table 5.2 that white wash and polished aluminium have nearly equal reflectivity but the emissivity of whitewash is much greater than that of aluminium. When exposed to solar radiation or to a clear night sky, whitewash will be cooler because of its higher emissivity. But when exposes to long wave radiation, aluminium will be cooler than whitewash because of its greater reflectivity of long wave radiation. Generally, it can be stated that light coloured surfaces stay cooler than dark surfaces and therefore in hot climates building surfaces should be painted in near white colours.

5.6.2 Insulation

Under steady state conditions the heat flow through a building element is proportional to its thermal conductance (U-value). Strictly speaking the steady state condition is never obtained in practice as outside conditions do change continuously to a greater or lesser extent, but the concept can be useful in determining the thermal performance of air conditioned buildings in temperate and humid climates. Under non steady state conditions which are found in building without mechanical heating or cooling in all climates and even for air conditioned buildings in hot day climates, apart from its U-value, the thermal capacity of the element also determines the heat flow and the "thermal diffusivity", "time-lag" and "decrement factor" become important. Time lag and decrement factor are both properties of the building element and not of the building materials. For building elements of massive construction the time lag is larger and the decrement factor smaller than for a light weight element, even through both may have the same U-value. The effect of massive construction is to lower the maximum internal day time temperature and to raise the minimum night time temperature while in light weight construction, the internal temperatures follow closely the pattern of outdoor temperatures. In warm climates with a large diurnal range it is advantageous to use massive building elements. The uncomfortable night time conditions in such structures can be modified by introducing additional night time ventilation. As no single material possesses all the desirable structural and thermal properties, combinations of materials with different properties are used to provide the necessary properties in an element. In such cases the time lag and decrement factor are also determined by the specific order in which the different layers are placed. Resistance insulation placed outside a brick wall given substantially higher time lag and lower decrement factor (Table 5.2) than if the same insulation is placed on the inner side of the wall. High time lag and low decrement factor are two important cooling concepts used in Rajasthan.

Table 5.2: Factor and time lag for different walls and roofs (after Dreyfus cited by Givoni, 1969)

Component	Composition (from exterior to interior)		Decrement factor	Time lag
Roof	Rockwool	4 cm	0.046	11h 50m
	Concrete	10 cm		
Roof	Concrete	10 cm	0.45	3h
	Rockwool	4 cm		
Wall	Plaster	15 cm		
	Concrete	10 cm		
	Air space		0.073	10h
	Concrete	10 cm		
	Plaster	15 cm		

Wall	Plaster	1.5 cm		
	Hollow concrete blocks	10 cm		
	Air space		0.056	10h 50m
	Hollow concrete blocs	10 cm		
	Plaster	1.5 cm		
Wall	Plaster	1.5 cm		
	Hollow bricks	10 cm	0.10	8h 45m
	Air space			
	Hollow bricks	10 cm		
	Plaster	1.5 cm		
Wall	Concrete	15 cm		
	Ventilated air space		0.073	10h
	concrete	15 cm		

Air cavities can be used in place of resistance insulation. By ventilating these cavities to the outside at certain times of the day or during a particular season their resistance value can be decreased with benefit. Used in this way, air cavities can create a wall or roof element with variable resistance. A similar effect is achieved by applying movable insulation, although at much greater cost.

5.7 HEAT REMOVAL FROM THE BUILDING

In spite of the most favourable arrangement of building form and building elements, some heat will reach the interior of the building. As a result of cooking, artificial lighting, use of machines etc., heat is generated within the building also. Therefore, suitable methods need to be employed to remove heat from the building interior. These methods can be broadly classified according to the principal heat sink used in them i.e. ground, air or night sky.

5.7.1 Ground

The diurnal variations of air temperature affect only the top 30 cm of soil and even the seasonal temperature variations are not felt below a few metres depth. The temperature deep, underground remains more or less constant throughout the year and for a given climate and soil conductivity, the constant temperature value depends upon the nature of the ground surface, the lowest values resulting from a shaded and irrigated surface (Bhardwaj, 1982). For Delhi, this value has been determined by Bhardwaj at 18^{0}C at 4 metres depth. If the building is constructed at this depth below the ground surface, it would be naturally cooled in summer and naturally heated in winter. Because of structural, drainage, damp-proofing and other problems it is not usually possible to construct buildings at such a depth. An alternative method is to construct tunnels at the appropriate depth (Fig. 5.10) and to cool air by blowing it through the tunnels. The cooled air is then used to condition living spaces in a normal building above the ground. Thoburn (1961) has reported the results for such a naturally air conditioned hospital building at Mathura.

Single story building can make better use of conductive heat loss to the ground. Such buildings can be partially buried under the soil either by building them at a lower level or by raising earth berms around a building constructed above the ground surface. Usually such buildings are also protected by a 30 to 60 cm earth layer above the roof. When planted with grass such a roof surface can be very effective in keeping the building cool (Nayak, 1982).

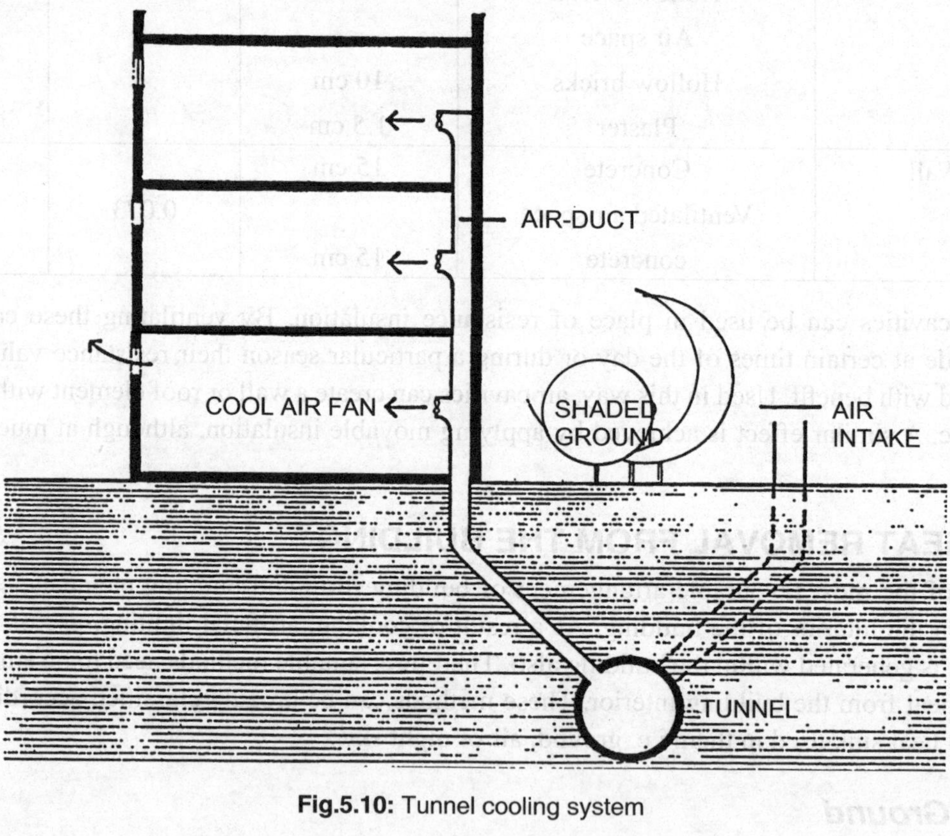

Fig.5.10: Tunnel cooling system

5.7.2 Air

Air as a heat sink is available mainly at night, when its temperature falls within the comfort range. During the cooler hours, outside air can be circulated through the building to help in cooling the structure. During the day time when the air is uncomfortably war, it can be used as a heat sink only by evaporating water on the building surface.

Ventilation of living spaces is necessary for removal of odours and gases produced by normal metabolic functions of the human body also. But the need for such ventilation is usually much less than that required for structural cooling and for ensuring human thermal comfort in warm or humid conditions. Hygienic ventilation is needed all the time while structural and comfort ventilation is useful only when the outdoor air temperature is lower than that indoors. In case it is possible to cool the air before it enters living spaces, structural and comfort ventilation can be used continuously also.

Natural ventilation of a building results from differential air pressure caused by wind incident on the various building surfaces and from thermal effects due to temperature differences between the outside and inside air. Factors such as surrounding landscape, location of other buildings, the building form and orientation with respect to prevailing wind direction, size and proportion of window openings and arrangement on internal partitions etc. affect both the quantity and pattern of wind induced air flow within the building. The thermally induced air movement depends upon the difference of indoor and outdoor air temperature, the size of inlet and outlet openings and the extent of vertical separation between such openings. These effects have been reviewed in detail by Givoni (196) and Van Straaten (1969) (Fig 5.11).

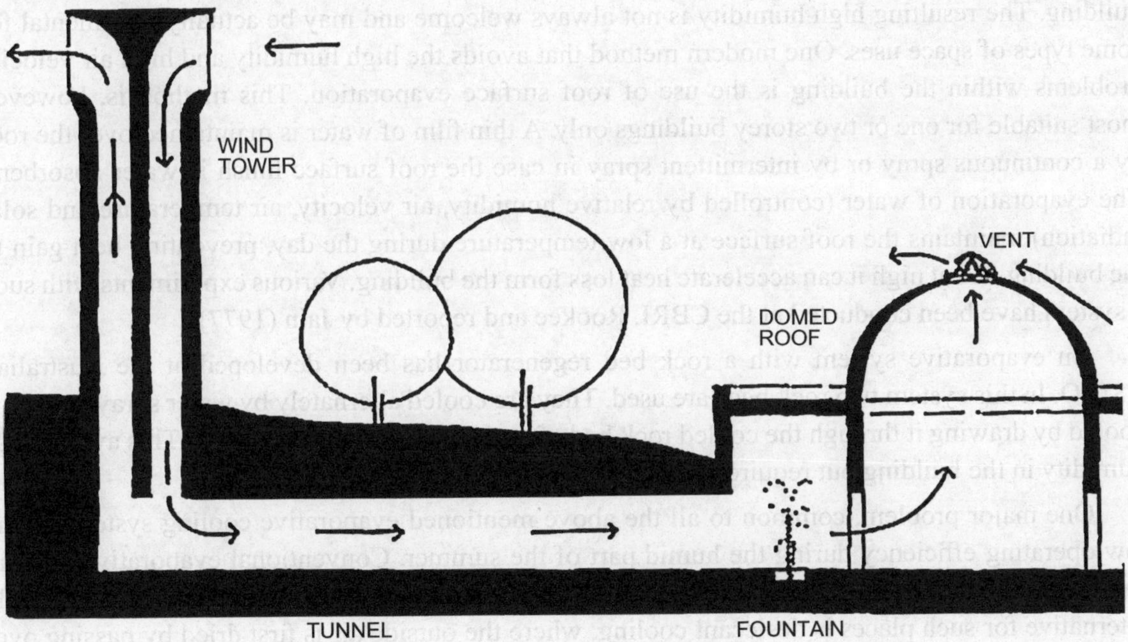

Fig.5.11: Wind towers used in Iran

Ventilation due to wind forces is of a higher order than due to thermal forces, but due to the intermittent nature of wind movement, the former type of ventilation cannot be ensured at the most appropriate times. In densely build urban areas, the effect of wind is considerably less than in open countryside or in sparsely built suburban area. The ensure ventilation in dense urban areas, therefore, the building layout must augment the thermal air flow. In most traditional towns, this is achieved by building around open spaces with varying degree of exposure to the sun. the 'courtyard effect' due to uneven heating of the open spaces, causes air to flow through the building. In certain cases wind scoops (Rudofsky, 1964) or tall towers (Bahadori, 1979) have been used to deflect winds from higher levels down into the building. It is usual in such buildings to provide some method to cool down the air before it reaches the living spaces. In the Iranian wind towers (Bahadori, 1978) the large thermal mass of the tower is used to cool the air during day time and to warm it at night. The wind scoops in Sind incorporate an evaporative cooling system.

The use of evaporative cooling is possible only in those areas where an adequate water supply is available in summer. This is generally difficult to ensure in hot dry climates. Evaporative cooling has been used for limited spaces in many traditional building. Grass mats hung in front of windows were sprinkled with water in Delhi (Gupta, 1981), earthen pitcher filled with water were used in Baghdad (Koenigsberger, 1971) underground streams were used in Iran (Baadori, 1978) fountains and water cascades were used in many palatial buildings in India. In recent times the window unit evaporative cooler consisting of an electrical fan and grass mat pads kept wet with or without a water pump has been used extensively in many countries. The major difficulty with such a device is the large volume of air (and consequently high indoor air velocity) that must move through the building. The resulting high humidity is not always welcome and may be actually detrimental for some types of space uses. One modern method that avoids the high humidity and high air velocity problems within the building is the use of roof surface evaporation. This method is, however, most suitable for one or two storey buildings only. A thin film of water is maintained over the roof by a continuous spray or by intermittent spray in case the roof surface finish is water absorbent. The evaporation of water (controlled by relative humidity, air velocity, air temperature and solar radiation) maintains the roof surface at a low temperature during the day, preventing heat gain to the building and at nigh it can accelerate heat loss form the building. Various experiments with such a system have been conducted at the CBRI, Rookee and reported by Jain (1977).

An evaporative system with a rock bed regenerator has been developed at the Australian CSIRO. In this system two rock beds are used. They are cooled alternately by water spray and air is cooled by drawing it through the cooled rock bed after the water spray is stopped. This avoids high humidity in the building but requires two fans and some ducting.

One major problem, common to all the above mentioned evaporative cooling systems is the low operating efficiency during the humid part of the summer. Conventional evaporative cooling cannot be used at all in regions where the humidity remains high throughout the year. A conceivable alternative for such places is desiccant cooling, where the outside air is first dried by passing over a desiccant material like silica gel and then cooled by evaporation. Solar energy can be used for regenerating the spent desiccant. In the Altenkrich house (Dannies, 1959) built in Israel in the fifties, desiccans were used as an integral part of the building which was oriented so that its long axis lay along the north south direction. The hollow east and west walls were filled with a sorbent material which permitted air flow through it. Evaporative coolers were placed on top of both walls and dampers were so arranged that air could flow through either wall from top to bottom or vice versa. During the forenoon while the sun was shining on the east wall, outdoor air was dried and cooled in the west wall. During the afternoon the spent sorbent material in the west wall was regenerated by sunshine and at this time air cooling was done by the east wall. Unfortunately, this interesting system of cooling has not been developed further after the initial experiments. The major difficulty with all desiccant cooling systems has been the non availability of suitable desiccants.

5.7.3 Night Sky

External building surface are constantly losing heat to the cool sky by radiation but during day time when the sun is shining, there is a net radiant heat gain to the surface. The atmosphere being opaque to long wave radiation except in the wave lengths 8 to 13 μm, much of the radiated heat gets reflected back to earth even at night. The radiant cooling potential of a building can therefore be improved by using external surface finishes that are efficient emitters in the wave length region 8 to 13 μm and are good reflectors for solar radiation (Catalonotti, 1975). Although such finishes are not available radiative cooling potential of building surfaces can be and has been used for space cooling.

Vertical building elements such as walls see only a part of the sky and therefore the radiative heat exchange between the building and sky takes place mainly through the roof. As the warm roof surface gets cooled by convection and radiation a stage is reached when the surface temperature equals the ambient air temperature. Further cooling by radiation continues but the cooling process is slower because the surface begins to gain heat by convection. If the net heat exchange reduces the roof temperature to the wet bulb temperature of the ambient air, atmospheric moisture begins to condense on the surface and no further cooling occurs. Thus radiative cooling potential is limited by the wet bulb temperature of air. The air in contact with the roof which gets cooled by convection (warming the roof in the process) can be collected and used for space cooling. In traditional buildings with courtyards, the cool air flows into the courtyard and then into the building. For this propose, the roof surfaces are sloped towards the internal courtyard and a parapet is raised around the roof to prevent mixing of the cool air with the warm outdoor air (Fig. 5.12).

Givoni (1969) has tested two methods of preventing connective heat gain to the radiatively cooled roof surface. In the first method the roof surface was covered by a layer of polythene which is transparent to long wave radiation. Cooled air is thus trapped between the roof surface and the polythene, from where it is taken directly into the building through openings in the roof. The problem of short life span of polythene was sought to be removed in the second method where the plastic cover was replaced by a white painted corrugated metal sheet which then became the radiative surface. For obvious reasons, the second method is more permanent but less effective.

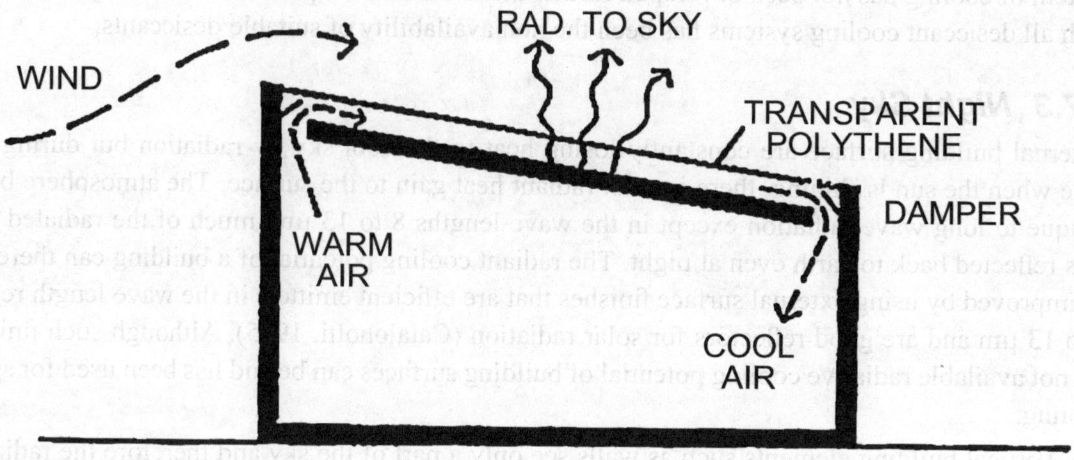

Fig.5.12: Roof radiation cooling system

Hay and Yellott (1970) also use the radiative cooling potential in the "skytherm" system. The roof is covered by a pond or a water filled plastic bag (Fig. 5.13) which is kept covered with insulation during day time. At nigh the insulation is removed and the water is allowed to cool down by evaporation and radiation. During the next day the water acts as a heat sink for the living space below, keeping it cool. This is an expensive system and its cost can be justified only if it is used for winter heating also (Gupta, 1979).

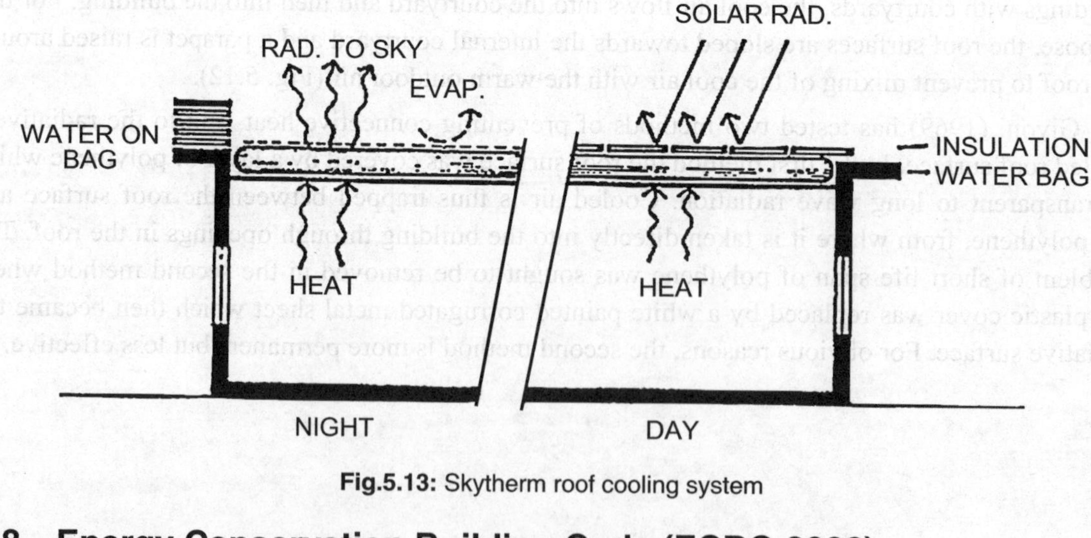

Fig.5.13: Skytherm roof cooling system

5.8 Energy Conservation Building Code (ECBC-2006)

5.8.1 Purpose

The purpose of this code is to provide minimum requirements for the energy-efficient design and construction of buildings.

5.8.2 Scope

The code is mandatory for commercial buildings or building complexes that have a connected load of 500 kW or greater or a contract demand of 600 kVA or greater. The code is also applicable to all buildings with a conditioned floor area of 1,000 m^2 (10,000 ft^2) or greater. The code is recommended for all other buildings.

5.8.2.1 Applicable Building Systems

The provisions of this code apply to:

a. Building envelopes, except for unconditioned storage spaces or warehouses,
b. Mechanical systems and equipment, including heating, ventilating, and air conditioning,
c. Service hot water heating,
d. Interior and exterior lighting, and
e. Electrical power and motors.

5.8.2.2 Exemptions

The provisions of this code do not apply to:

a. Buildings that do not use either electricity or fossil fuel,
b. Equipment and portions of building systems that use energy primarily for manufacturing processes, and
c. Multi-family buildings of three or fewer stories above grade, and single-family buildings.

5.8.2.3 Safety, Health and Environmental Codes Take Precedence

Where this code is found to conflict with safety, health, or environmental codes, the safety, health, or environmental codes shall take precedence.

5.8.3 Administration and Enforcement

5.8.3.1 Compliance Requirements

5.8.3.2 Mandatory Requirements

Compliance with the requirements of this energy code shall be mandatory for all applicable buildings discussed in 2.

5.8.3.3 New Buildings

New buildings shall comply with either the provisions of 4 through 8 of this code or the Energy Budget Method of 10.

5.8.3.4 Additions to Existing Buildings

Where the addition plus the existing building exceeds the conditioned floor area threshold of 2, additions shall comply with the provisions of 4 through 8. Compliance may be demonstrated in either of the following ways:

a. The addition alone shall comply with the applicable requirements, or

b. The addition, together with the entire existing building, shall comply with the requirements of this code that would apply to the entire building, as if it were a new building.

Exception to 3.1.3: When space conditioning is provided by existing systems and equipment, the existing systems and equipment need not comply with this code. However, any new equipment installed must comply with specific requirements applicable to that equipment.

5.8.3.5 Alterations to Existing Buildings

Where the existing building exceeds the conditioned floor area threshold in 2, portions of a building and its systems that are being altered shall meet the provisions of 4 through 8. The specific requirements for alterations are described in the following subsections.

Exception to 3.1.4: When the entire building complies with all of the provisions of 4 through 8 as if it were a new building.

5.8.3.6 Building Envelope

Alterations to the building envelope shall comply with the requirements of 4 for fenestration, insulation, and air leakage applicable to the portions of the buildings and its systems being altered.

Exception to 3.1.4.1: The following alterations need not comply with these requirements provided such alterations do not increase the energy usage of the building:

a. Replacement of glass in an existing sash and frame, provided the U-factor and SHGC of the replacement glazing are equal to or lower than the existing glazing,

b. Modifications to roof/ceiling, wall, or floor cavities, which are insulated to full depth with insulation, and

c. Modifications to walls and floors without cavities and where no new cavities are created.

5.8.3.7 Heating, Ventilation and Air Conditioning

Alterations to building heating, ventilating, and air-conditioning equipment or systems shall comply with the requirements of 5 applicable to the portions of the building and its systems being altered. Any new equipment or control devices installed in conjunction with the alteration shall comply with the specific requirements applicable to that equipment or control device.

5.8.3.8 Service Water Heating

Alterations to building service water heating equipment or systems shall comply with the requirements of 6 applicable to the portions of the building and its systems being altered. Any new equipment or control devices installed in conjunction with the alteration shall comply with the specific requirements applicable to that equipment or control device.

5.8.4 Solar Passive Architecture

- Solar Passive Architecture design uses a building form and fabric to capture, store and distribute solar energy thereby reducing the demand for artificial lighting, cooling and heating.

- It consists of sitting the building so that large glazed area can face south and incorporating energy efficiency features such as, adequate roof and wall insulation.
- The adoption of solar passive techniques can make important contribution to reducing the energy requirements of non domestic buildings such as officers, schools and factories.
- In commercial building lighting accounts for a major portion of the total energy requirement and significant opportunities exits for achieving savings through the optimum use of daylight.
- Daylight is greatly under utilized resource. Careful building design can provide comfortable levels of even interior lighting without glare and yield sufficient saving in electricity consumption to reduce need for artificial light.

5.8.4.1 Active solar technology

- Active Solar Systems involve the use of collectors to capture heat from the sun and heat transfer medium such as water or oil circulated. Active solar systems are used for water heating and space heating and cooling.
- Photovoltaic system converts solar radiation to direct current electricity by the interaction of photons.
- Advantages
- Decentralized power generation
- No T&D losses
- Saving of fossil fuels
- Environment friendly resources

5.8.4.2 Salient features

Unique floating slab system to allow free and quick movement of air

- Solar chimenies to accelerate the quick drafting of hot air.
- Cavity walls with and without insulation for thermal comfort
- Light vaults in the south to admit light without glare and heat
- Hyperbolic shell roof over central atrium designed to admit daylight without glare and heat
- Insulated roof for thermal comfort
- Wind tower in the Central Atrium for scientific cooling
- 25Kwp Solar Photo voltaic power plant integrated to meet the basic requirements of the building.
- Designed landscaping and horticulture work
- Water bodies with water falls and fountains.

(i) Solar Chimney

Solar chimney is a collector panel which absorbs the incident solar radiation and heats up the air in the absorber glazing space. In winter the hot air forces itself into the living space through the vents and heats it up. Cool air takes its place and the cycle is repeated. Summer cooling can be realized by venting out the hot air and providing another opening for replacing the hot air by cool air from a shaded or cooler area.

(ii) WindTower

Wind towers are generally used for cooling purposes. A pre-requisite for using a wind tower is that the site should experience winds with a fairly good and consistent velocity. A wind tower operates in various ways, according to the time of day and the presence and absence of wind. The principle behind its operation lies in changing the temperature and thereby density of the air in and around the tower. The difference in density creates a draft, pulling the air either upwards or downwards through the tower.

(iii) Solar passive complex of PEDA

- The aim of construction of solar passive complex is to encourage the commercial integration of passive solar design into buildings.
- PEDA is setting up demonstration building with the intention to determine, present and publicist the substantial benefits that drive from passive solar technology not only in relation to energy performance but also in terms of environmental and aesthetic qualities usually prevailing in passive solar buildings.

(iv) Details of Complex

Location	:	Sector 33D, Chandigarh
Climate	:	Composite
Plot size	:	268' x 243' (1.49 acre)
Area Statement		
Ground floor	:	24760 sq. ft
Reception		
Central Atrium		
Office		
Exhibition centre		
Auditorium		
Cafeteria		
Upper ground floor	:	7370 sq.ft
First floor	:	11,308 sq. ft.

Second floor	:	3552 sq. ft.
Basement floor	:	23688
Total covered area	:	70306 sq.ft.
Ground coverage	:	26598 sq.ft
Estimated cost	:	Rs. 550 lacs
Schedule date of completion		December 2004

The hot ambient air coming in contact with the cool top part of the tower is cooled. It becomes cold and dense, and sinks through the tower and into the living spaces, replacing the hot air. In the presence of wind, the air is cooled more effectively and flows faster down the tower and into the living area. In the absence of wind, the downward flow ceases and the tower begins to act like a chimney. Operation of tower depends greatly on ambient fluctuations like the wind velocity, air, temperature, changes etc.

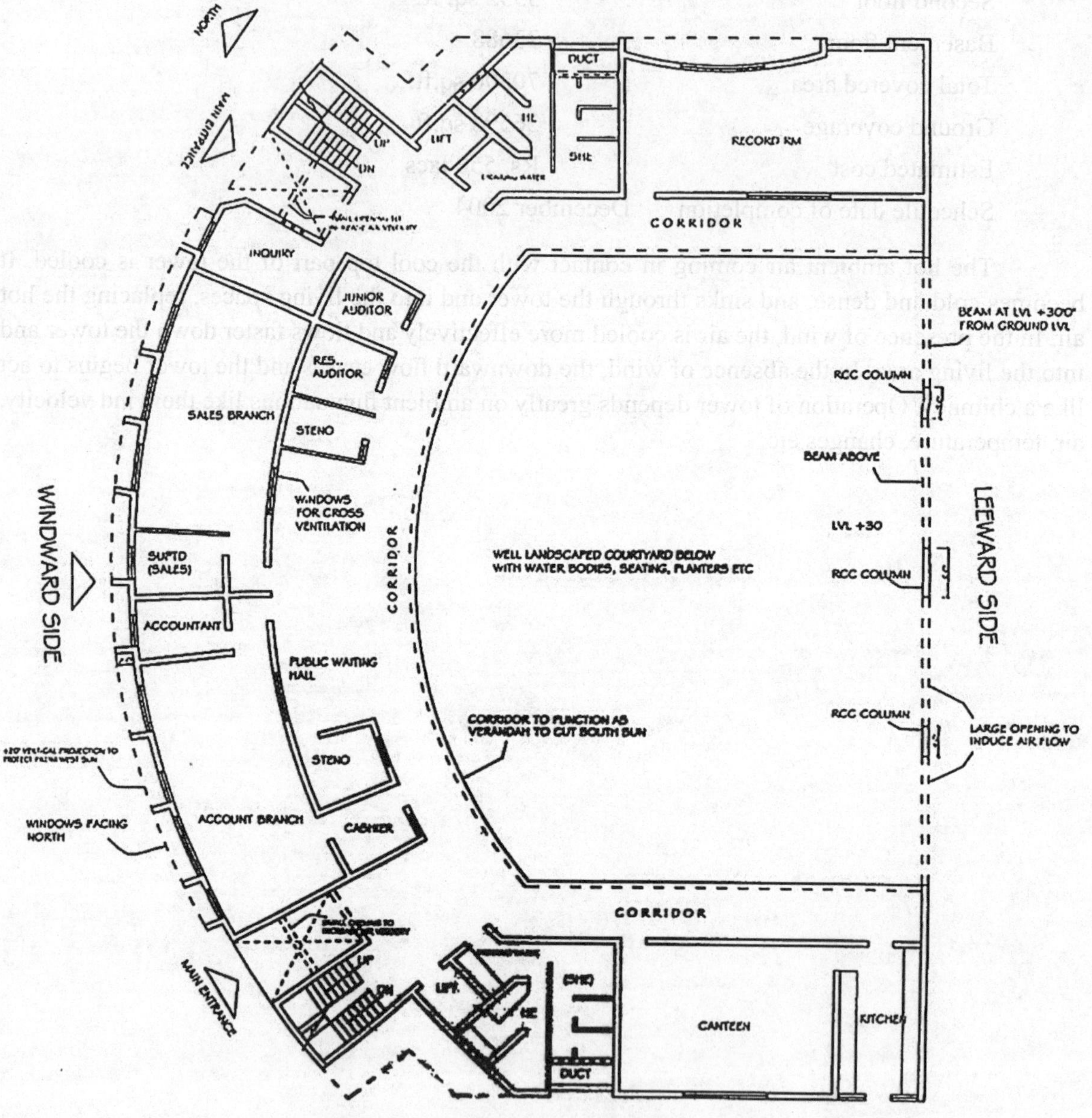

Fig.5.14: Ground floor plan of PEDA building

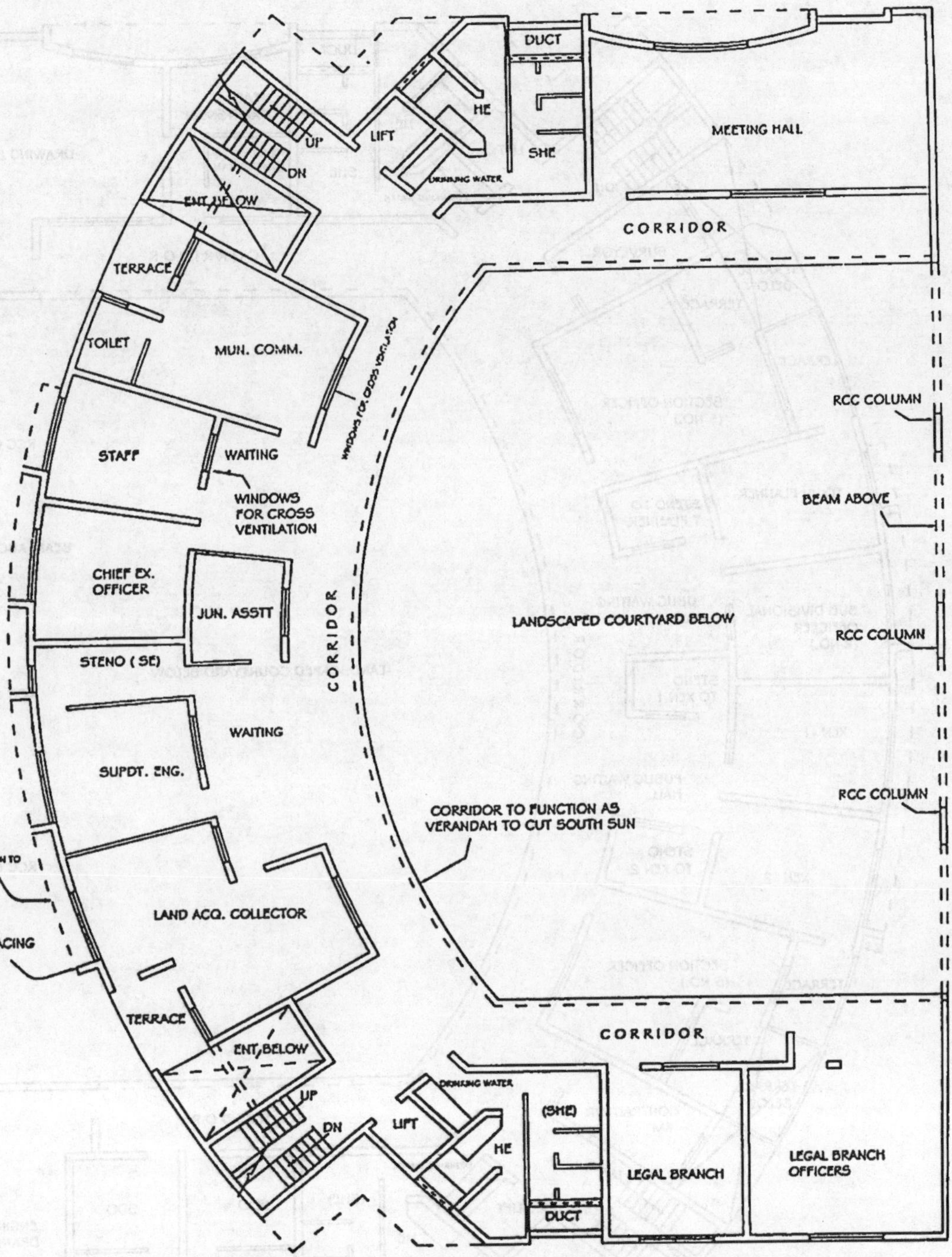

Fig.5.15: Firs floor plan of PEDA building

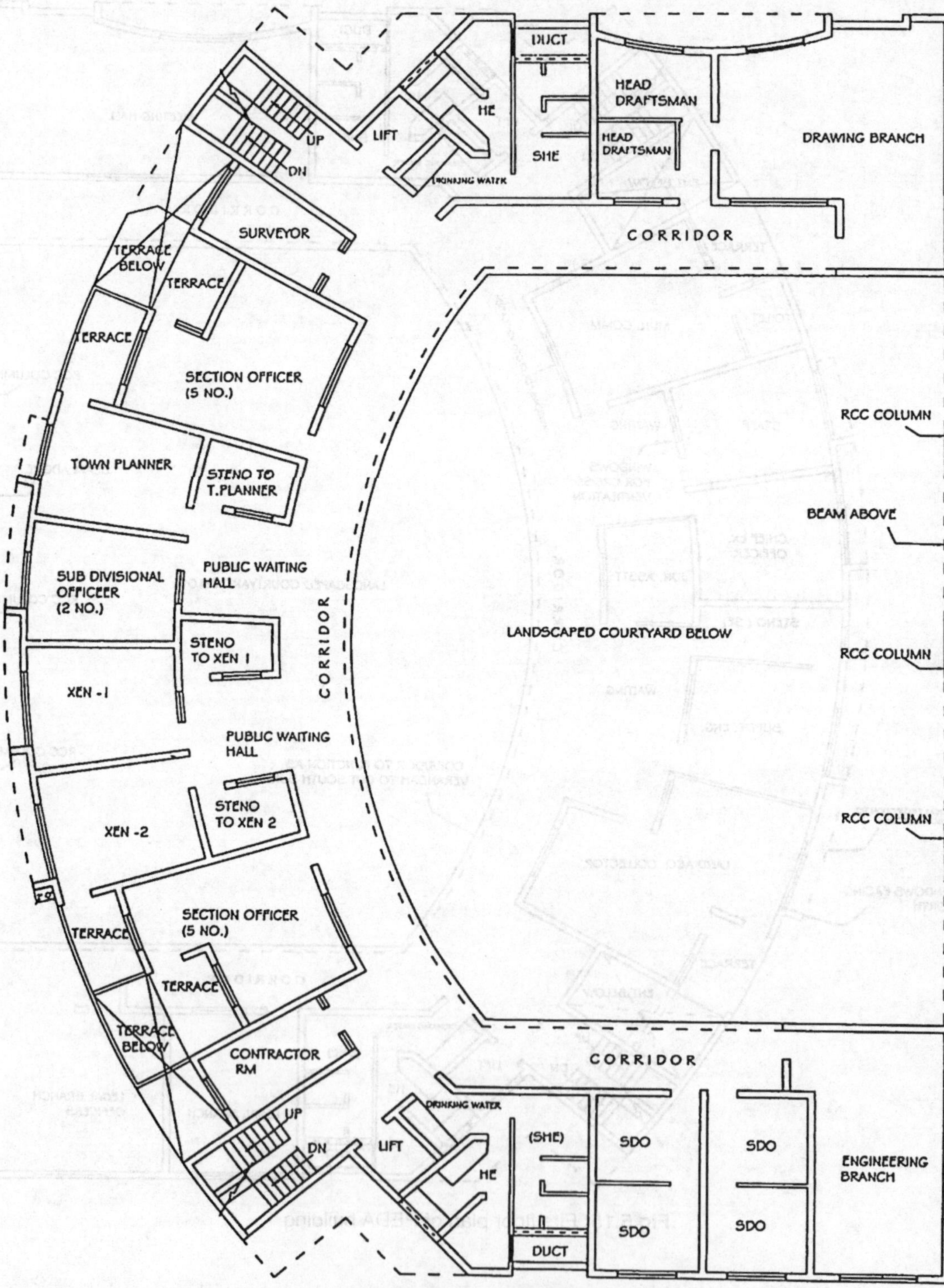

Fig.5.16: Second floor plan of PEDA building

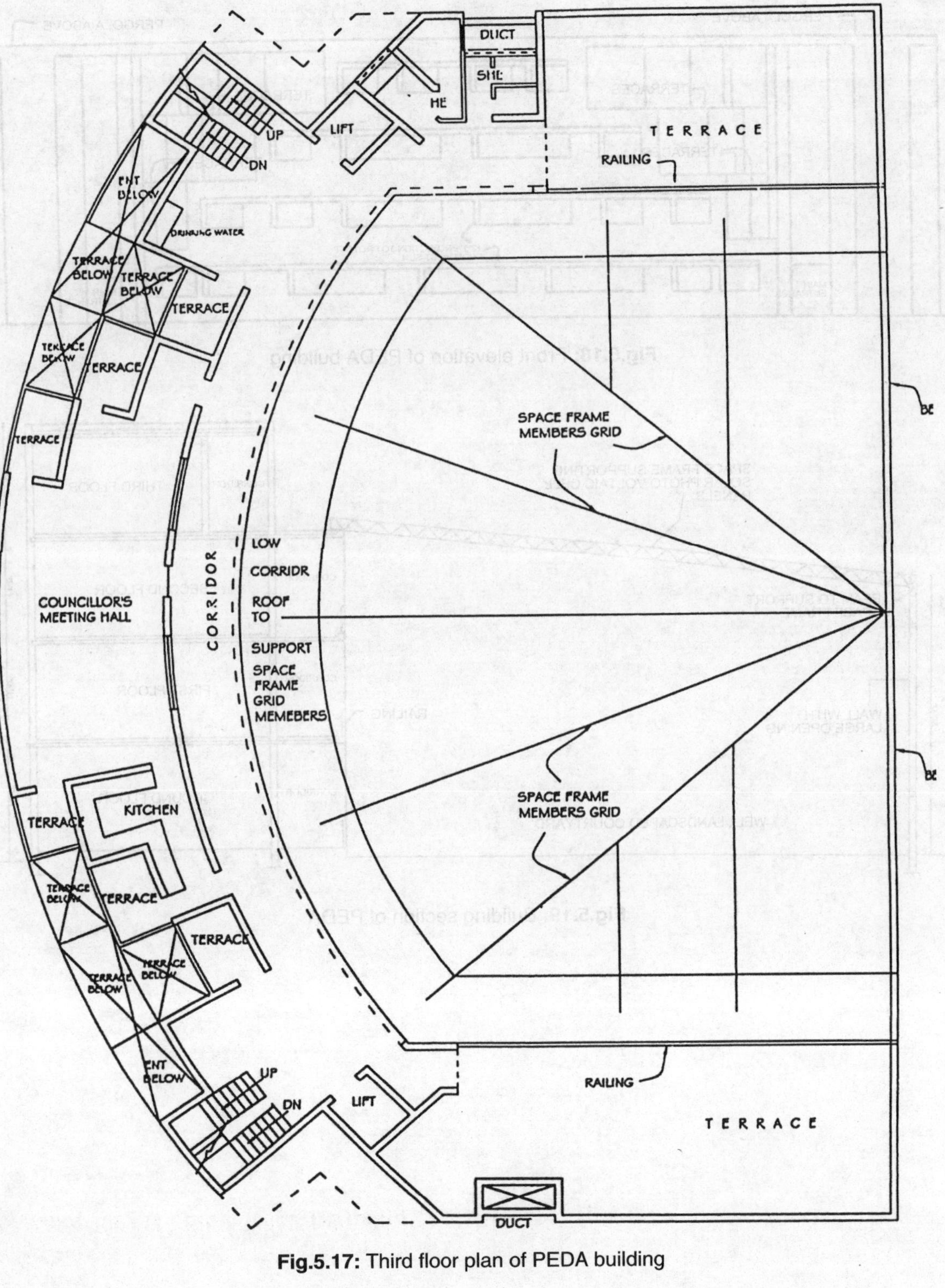

Fig.5.17: Third floor plan of PEDA building

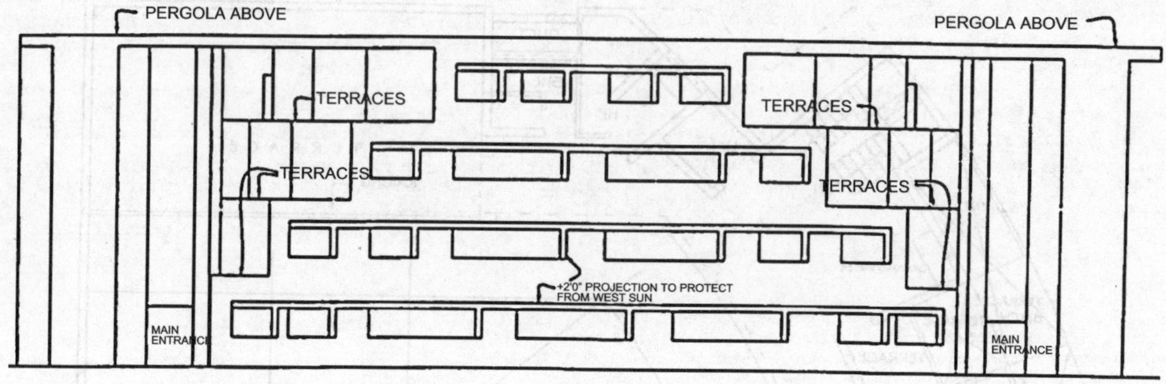

Fig.5.18: Front elevation of PEDA building

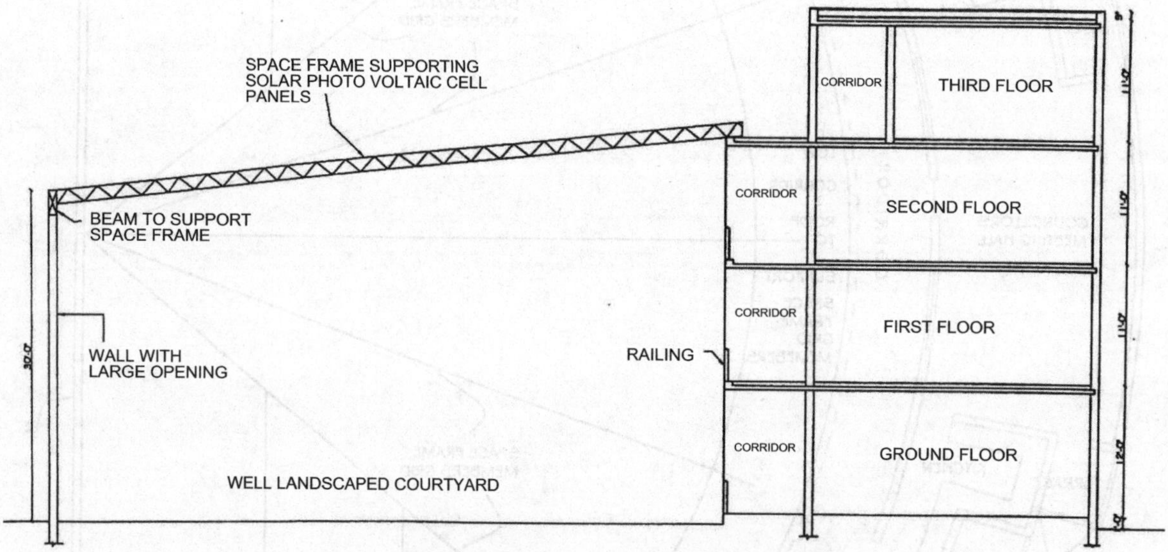

Fig.5.19: Building section of PEDA

6 Energy Auditing and Radiation Cooling of Buildings in Hot and Dry Climate

6.1 Energy Auditing

The dictionary variously defines the word audit as "a form examination and variation of financial accounts" "an methodological examination and review" or "an examination wit intent to verify". Energy audit is akin to financial audit, because finance is one among the several resources in the manufacturing process, energy being the other.

Energy audit can alternatively be defined as a systematic study, carried out to identify the wasteful practices and means of improving energy efficiency in order to reduce energy consumption. Energy audit is an essential tool for energy conservation it is considered as a "Hidden resources". Since the opportunities are plenty for energy conservation. But more often than not these are not known to the management or it these are known, are not in thematic towards their implementation. Hairs from implementing the energy conservation studies can be substantial. A study carried out by NPC (National Productivity Council) has reported saving potential of 10 to 25% in Indian Industry. The purpose of energy audit is to evaluate and provide essential ingredients for successful energy conservation programme. It identifier opportunities for financial saving by elimination of wasteful use of electricity, cool, fuel oil etc. without attesting the process or quality of production.

The energy audit encompassed the following aspects:

i. Site survey of the plant and study of plant layout, civil drawings, single line diagrams etc.
ii. Interview of plant official about general operating conditions of plants.
iii. Comprehensive measurement of selected plant items like electrical parameters, exhaust gas composition, radiation losses various temperatures, oil and water how etc.
iv. Calculation and analysis of measured and collected data and establishment of energy and material balances.
v. Identification of potential areas of energy conservation and measures for the same.
vi. Financial analysis of identified measures to examine techno-economic feasibility.

An energy audit is conducted in the plant with the sole aim of reducing cost of production by reducing every cost.

An energy audit is now a requirement for non domestic buildings so that a Building Energy Certificate can be prepared.

An energy audit attempts to allocate a value at each point of energy consumption over a given period, usually a year. It should at the least allocate a value to the consumption of the various forms of energy on site. Following an energy audit it should then be possible to identify at each points of energy consumption the corresponding of the various forms of energy on site. Following an energy audit it should then be possible to identify at each points of energy consumption the corresponding energy demand. This may require an analysis of energy demand at each point. The difference between energy consumption and energy demand can then be addressed and ways considered to reduce it at each point to its smallest practical value.

The relationship between energy consumption, AEC and annual energy demand AED is as AEC = AED (seasonal efficiency)^{kWh}.

6.1.1 Preliminaries to an Energy Audit

Before proceeding with an energy audit it is essential the a survey of the staff who use the buildings in undertaken to establish if the comfort levels are acceptable during the winter season and to find out if the provision of hot water for consumption is adequate. It is not uncommon in a survey of this kind to find that complains arise due to discomfort from the lack of adequate space heating. This may be due to variety of reasons. The effect this will have on the energy audit may will be significant as it will shown a false annual energy consumption.

If the standard of comfort in thee areas of complaint are addressed after the audit, there will be an increase in annual energy consumption in the following year. This will give a negative signal to the client or senior management. If the complaints of cover heating are found as evidenced by over windows on cold days this could be the first issue to be addressed in the programme of energy conservation that follows the audit. For sedentary occupation in modern well insulated buildings the majority of people will be neither uncomfortably warm in winter in rooms where the dry resultant temperature is between 19 and 23^{0}C.

6.1.2 Outcomes of the Energy audit

Clearly if the efficiency of energy utilization can be improved, the difference between AED and AEC will be reduced and seasonal efficiency will be increased.

The efficiency of energy use in the case of boiler plant for space heating and the provision of hot water supply over a period will be its seasonal efficiency. Modern at converting primary energy than older plant. There have been significant advances in boiler and burner design. New plant like the condensing boiler which has a very high efficiency has entered the market in recent years. There are however, other ways in which annual energy consumption can be reduced and these involve an equally valid approach, namely reduce the annual demand for energy.

By reducing AED, AEC should also be reduced. There are a variety of action points have and they include:

- Checking maintenance schedules and certificates to ensure that plant and system preventive maintenance has been under taken.
- Checking time scheduling of plants and zones.
- Checking there no state settings.
- Checking the thermal insulation on distribution mains.
- Identify and costing potential energy saving from improvement in the thermal insulation of the building.
- Identifying and costing reduction of ingress of necessary outdoor air into entrance areas and corridors via entrance doors, stair wells and life wells and around windows.
- Encouraging the occupants of the building to view energy conservation as a daily habit.

The last action point is perhaps the most important. The education of staff in an awareness of energy conservation is paramount to the success of energy conservation initiative. The energy audit does not of itself reduce energy use on a site. It can however assist in initiating action to reduce the annual energy cost. The energy audit therefore provides two potential courses of action :

- Improving the efficiency of energy utilization to reduce the differences between AED and AEC to its lowest paraxial value.
- To reduce annual energy demand to its lowest practical value.

6.1.3 Measurement of Primary Energy Consumption

In order to prepare an energy audit the invoices for all primary energy supplied to site must be available for at least the penultimate calendar year. Adjustment may have to be made to ensure that the invoices for different fuel cover the same period. The use of estimated readings should be avoided or checked. At the same time the client should be encouraged to have various fuels used on site accurately metered so that the fuel accounts for the following year are precise.

Measurement of the consumption of electricity, gas and bulk fuels such as petrol, diesel oil, heating oil, coal, bottled prepare and butane can be monitored at the incoming point on site for each. However, the client should be advised to meter the fuels and energy consumption at the various points of use so that in time a more detailed energy audit at points of use can be undertaken.

6.1.4 Primary Energy Tariffs

One of the responsibilities of an energy manager is the negotiation of tariffs with the privatized utilities. It is not within the scope of this book to provide advise in this area that has now become quite specifised. There is no doubt however, that negotiation of competitive tariffs will have a bearing upon the annual cost of energy, but it is a one off procedure at least until the tariffs come up of renegotiation. It is therefore only one of many other potential energy, conservation measures. Energy conservation features to take into account when investigating the energy supply markets are:

- Annual base load requirement
- Peak load and their frequency and point of occurrence
- Penalties for exceeding peak loads (and ways this can be avoided by load shading)
- Seasonal load
- Security of supply (end potential need for back up supplies)
- In the consumption of electricity power factor correction

You can see that these features require detailed knowledge of the way primary energy is consumed on the site. This data may not be fully available from historical records and the energy manager may need to interview key occupants/employees for evidence at points of energy use.

Table 4.9:A format for an initial energy audit

S.No	Particular	Gas	Oil	Electricity	LPG	Total
1	Fuel					
2	Consumption (Liters, kWh, bottles)					
3	Consumption in kWh					
4	Annual cost (Rs.)					
5	Cost / kWh					
6	% Total cost					100
7	% Total consumption					100

Item (1) the table should show all types of energy used on the site.

Item (2) consumption should be based upon fuel invoices and best estimates where necessary

Item (3) consumption figures converted to a common unit either GJ or kWh

Item (4) the total annual cost of the energy / fuel inclusive of standing charges where appropriate

Item (5) item (4) item (3)

Item (6)Item (4) total lost in item (4)

Item (7) Item (3) total consumption in item (3)

Table 6.10: Energy conversion for common fuels

Fuel	Energy Produced	
	MJ	kWh
1 kg of coal (average)	27.4	7.61

1 litre of petrol	40	11.12
1 cubic meter of natural gas	33.7	10.76
1 cubic toot of natural gas	1.1	0.305
1 cubic meter of propane gas	92.6	25.72
1 kg of propane gas	50	13.9
1 litre of light fuel oil	40.5	4.26
1 litre of heavy fuel oil	41.5	11.44
1 kWh of electricity	3.6	1.0

6.1.5 Energy Audit Team

For any establishment in order to make an energy audit successful a multidisciplinary team is required which will cover all technical, safety, accountancy and management aspects. This is best accomplished by involving site personnel of suitable rank specializing in these aspects and bearing appropriate experience. An essential past of energy auditing is to establish a sound working relationship with the site personnel.

The audit team normally consists of (i) technical manpower (ii) floor manager/supervisor (iii) audit personnel along with a person called Energy Manager as team leader. The team leader should have general technical knowledge with lot of managerial skill. The technical manpower may consist of electrical, mechanical, electronics, instrumentation and civil engineers, floor manager/ supervisor may also have a draftsman in their team.

The energy audit team may comprise:

i. Works manager (team leader)
ii. Material manager
iii. Electrical / electronics engineers
iv. Mechanical engineer
v. Civil engineer
vi. Account officer / accountant
vii. Technician bearing knowledge of electrical / electronics / mechanical and computer awareness

6.2 Energy Management

The concept of energy conservation in building by utilizing intelligence to explore and exploit various resources for the benefit of mankind has started from being start of civilization. The concept of intelligent or green building had proper management has been developed through the proper use of information technology and energy auditing by which comfortable living condition can be achieved. This also helps to reduce the wastage of energy and optimum utilization of available resources. It has been shown that energy consumption for comfort in the buildings could be reduced even half by the proper use of equipments and efficient controls. Energy management is a moving feast it is still a young discipline and much of what is known has to be derived from historical data in the form of fuel invoices equated with building type, level of services specifications, level of building specifications and level of proactive and requirements of its concept the intelligent buildings which may defined as "one which provides a productive and cost effective environment through optimization of its four basic elements structure, systems, services and management and the inter relationship between them. Intelligent buildings help building owners, properly managers and occupants to realize their goals in the area of cost, comfort convenience, safety, long term flexibility and marketability.

6.2.1 Building Management System (BMS)

Building Management System (BMS) comprise of the creation of such an environment for the process taking place with the building that provides optimal functionality and integration of processes concerned. The concept of management in this case may be imagined as a control loop.

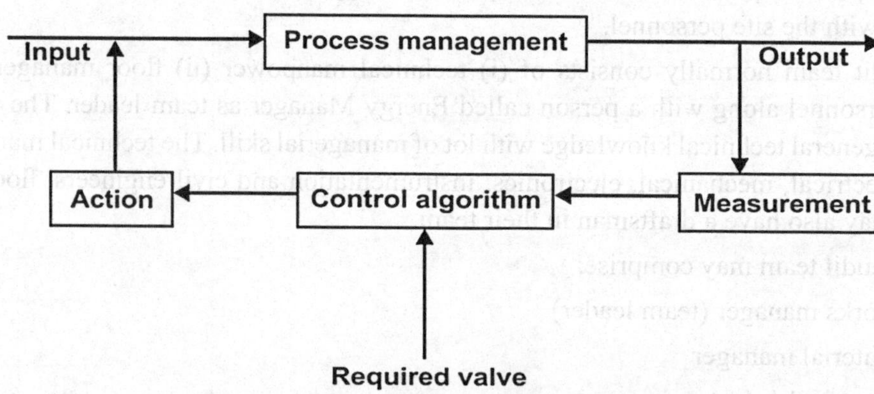

Fig.6.1: Building Management System

The objective to be managed in this case is the building or building complex that constituted the process. The input to this process is formed by the goods, the energy and services needed to keep the process going. The services provided by the building like accommodation, comfort, safely and security constitute the output of the process. To be able to keep this output at the required qualitative and quantitative levels the following condition have to be met.

- Methods are required for measuring the quantity and the quality of the output.
- Set points and standards are needed with which the desired quality and quantity of the output can be compared unambiguously.
- Means are needed for controlling the process or its input in order to be able to adjust the output.

As a building management system is in fact an information processing system, it should provide functions for data input, processing this data into information and get the result as output to the operator.

6.2.2 Energy Conservation Approaches

When we start considering energy conservation through building management we will examine all the facilities involved in meeting the above conditions. We have achieve the desired output with the optimization of the equipments involved in giving us the necessary inputs. We will look at the available new control products and improvement that might contribute to achieve our desired goal.

Energy conservation begins with the basic like thermostats, valves, dampers etc in heating, ventilation and air conditioning (HVAC) system with the building. Before starting the exploration and automation can do we have to given attention in renovating and modernizing various parts and equipments. A constant flow of creativity and imagination must be directed to the task of energy management. We can being immediately with some opportunities like:

- Cool the building at 24^{0}C when it is occupied and stop cooling when it is not occupied.
- Reduce the outside air ventilation from the conventional 0.2 cfm per square feet to 5-10 cfm per person where safety is not compromised.
- Change air filter on a regular schedule to ensure maximum cooling or heating capacity.
- Turn of non critical exhaust fans so that cooled / heated air is not exhausted unnecessarily.
- Reduce domestic not water temperatures to a comfortable level.
- Turn of lighting in unoccupied work areas, reduce lighting in corridors and stairways to 30 foot candles where safety rules are not disturbed.

Besides, these simple adjustments, just mentioned how shall we view the value of our investment of funds in energy conservation, versus the alternative possibilities. It takes money to make money so we have to invest money to save energy. To determine the real value of investment in energy conservation four things must be considered:

- The cost of energy
- The cost of implementing the energy management plan
- Occupant productivity and
- Pay back

The various approaches to address the situation to achieve the goal of energy conservation, a challenging goal through very much realistic method. Few of the approaches are:

6.2.3 Selection of Equipments

i. In HVAC dampers are used to control the flow of air. Standard damper can allow 5% to 30%. Leakage when it is closed. Through use of low leakage dampers we can restrict leakage to less than 1% to reduce this wasteful load.

ii. Through efficient control the outdoor air used in ventilation could be reduced to minimum level but definitely within the range of ASHRAE'S standard.

iii. Energy saving are possible by closing off outside ventilation air during unoccupied periods. Required ventilation for conditioned spaces need only be supplied while they are occupied. By the addition of time clock or automation system the outside air could be shut off during these unoccupied periods. The result is a lower demand on HVAC equipment to cool or heat that necessary outside air.

iv. Using outside air to cool a building can result in lower mechanical configuration cost whenever outdoor air has a lower heat content (enthalpy) than the return air. This can be accomplished by integrated economizer or enthalpy control.

v. Many systems using a hot deck and a cold deck rely on fixed hot deck / cold deck from outdoor temperature, leaving the old deck at a fixed temperature. none of the above control strategies takes actual zone loads into account,, and therefore wastes energy by missing air that is too hot with that is too cold. Money and energy can be saved by having hot deck temperature controls responds to the areas controls having the greatest heating demand. As the demand is reduced the hot deck temperature is lower accordingly reducing energy required by the hot deck energy supplied.

vi. Terminal reheat systems ordinarily use a fixed cold deck temperature and apply thermostat controlled reheat in each zone to maintain comfort. It every zone is reheating, the cold deck is too cold and cooling energy, as well as reheat energy is being wasted. Energy can be saved by installing zone optimizing load analyzer on the temperature controls. The demand of each zone is measured and cold supply air temperature is set upward to minimize the amount of reheat required. This makes the HVAC system flexible enough to satisfy the zone greatest demand and reduced the total amount of energy needed for both cooling and heating.

6.2.4 Management Aspects of Energy Conservation

- Preliminary energy use, survey and analysis along with development of an energy audit format.
- Continuous energy accounting, monitoring and arriving at energy audit results.
- Establishment of regular energy management reporting.
- Appointment of energy manager supported by an energy management committee.
- Appreciation programme for senior level executives and identification of broad energy management objectives.
- Investment decision for short term medium term and long term conservation measures.
- Evolution of appropriate training programmes for workers in the efficient use of energy.

6.2.5 Money Saving Tips for Domestic Consumers

- Switch off electrical appliances and lights when not in use.

- Keep lamps and fixtures free from dust and dirt.
- Use light colors for walls, ceilings, furniture and curtains.
- Use tube lights which give more light as compared to bulbs, consume less electricity and have a longer life.
- Close refrigerator door quickly.
- Don't open / close refrigerator doors very frequently.
- Use standard electrical fittings and fixtures.
- Use wires of proper size in house wiring to reduce loss of energy.
- Don't use remote control to switch of the TV or any other electrical gadget, instead switch them off from the mains, thus switching off the stabilizer supply.
- Use CFL in place of tube rods wherever possible.

6.2.6 Some Money Saving Tips to Industrial Consumers

- Lubricate motors and motor drives regularly to reduce friction.
- Keep the motors clean to help them cool properly.
- Place the motor as close to the load as possible.
- Match the motors to your requirement. Oversized motors waste energy.
- Use motors of high efficiency.
- Use shunt capacitors across motor terminals to reduce KVA charges and also avoid damage to motors.
- Tighten belt and pulley at regular intervals to reduce loss of energy due to slip.
- Replace worm out bearings immediately and ensure timely repairs.
- Make greater use of daylight.
- Improve power factor if necessary
- Use proper wiring for machines.
- Place the supply system properly at the load centre.

6.2.7 Some Tips for Managers to Save Electricity

- Turn-off all light other than those required for security when the building is unoccupied.
- Use tube rods in place of bulbs and CFL in place of tube rods wherever possible as they consume less electricity and have a longer life.
- Make greater use of daylight for illumination.
- Avoid use of decorative and diffused lighting.
- Decrease partition heights wherever possible.
- Turn-off water coolers at the end of normal business hours.

- Encourage all personnel to walk up and come down on flight of stairs, rather than using lift.
- Reduce the number of lifts in service during off-peak hours.
- Use energy efficient technology.

6.3 Radiation Cooling of buildings in hot and dry climate

6.3.1 Introduction

Heating and cooling account for 50 to 70% of the energy used in the average Indian home. Inadequate insulation and air leakage are leading causes of energy waste in most homes. Insulation:

- saves money and our nation's limited energy resources
- makes your house more comfortable by helping to maintain a uniform temperature throughout the house, and
- Makes walls, ceilings, and floors warmer in the winter and cooler in the summer.
- Implementation of measures for energy conservation & realization of savings

The amount of energy you conserve will depend on several factors: your local climate; the size, shape, and construction of your house; the living habits of your family; the type and efficiency of the heating and cooling systems; and the fuel you use. Once the energy savings have paid for the installation cost, energy conserved is money saved - and saving energy will be even more important as utility rates go up.

This fact sheet will help you to understand how insulation works, what different types of insulation are available, and how much insulation makes sense for your climate. There are many other things you can do to conserve energy in your home as well. The Department of Energy offers many web sites to help you save energy by sealing air leaks, selecting more energy-efficient appliances, etc.

Heat flows naturally from a warmer to a cooler space. In winter, the heat moves directly from all heated.

Living spaces to the outdoors and to adjacent unheated attics, garages, and basements - wherever there is a difference in temperature. During the summer, heat moves from outdoors to the house interior. To maintain comfort, the heat lost in winter must be replaced by your heating system and the heat gained in summer must be removed by your air conditioner. Insulating ceilings, walls, and floors decreases the heating or cooling needed by providing an effective resistance to the flow of heat Betts, blankets, loose fill, and low-density foams all work by limiting air movement.

(These products may be more familiarly called fiberglass, cellulose, polyicynene, and expanded polystyrene.) The still air is an effective insulator because it eliminates convection and has low conduction. Some foam, such as polyisocyanurate, polyurethane, and extruded polystyrene, are filled with special gases that provide additional resistance to heat flow.

Reflective insulation works by reducing the amount of energy that travels in the form of radiation. Some forms of reflective insulation also divide a space up into small regions to reduce air movement, or convection, but not to the same extent as bats, blankets, loose-fill, and foam.

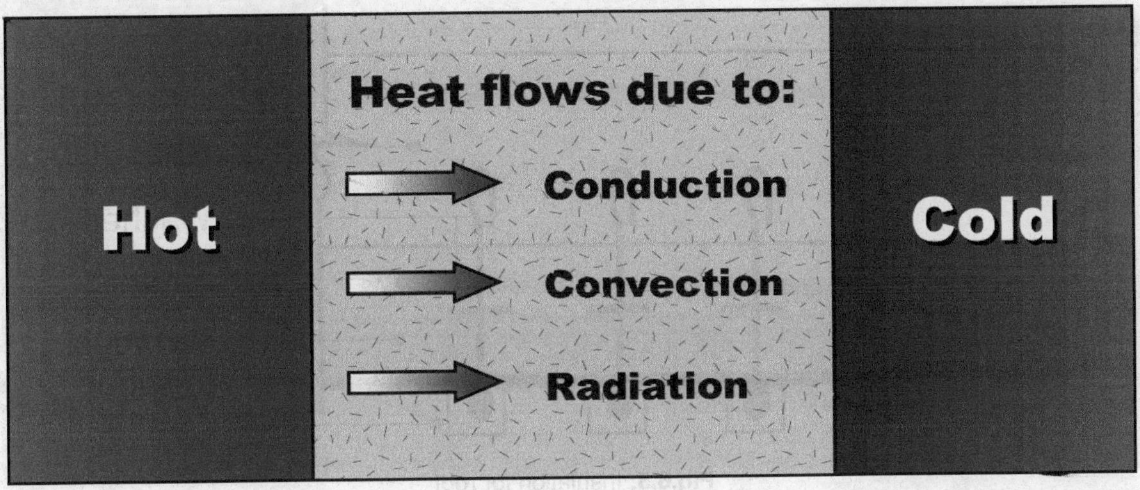

Fig.6.2: Heat flow in room

6.3.2 Steps to make room more energy efficient

The term **thermal insulation** can refer to materials used to reduce the rate of heat transfer, or the methods and processes used to reduce heat transfer. Heat energy can be transferred by conduction, convection, radiation or by actual movement of material from one location to another. For the purposes of this discussion only the first three mechanisms need to be considered. Thermal insulation is the method of preventing heat from escaping a container or from entering the container. In other words, thermal insulation can keep an enclosed area such as a building warm, or it can keep the inside of a container cold. Heat is transferred from one material to another by conduction, convection and/or radiation. Insulators are used to minimize that transfer of heat energy.

6.3.3 Insulation for roof

- Average hours of solar radiations – 8.2 hours (9.7 hours/day in May, 6.4 hours/day in August).
- About 50-65% a heat is transferred inside through roof, hence insulation of roof is essential.
- Figure 6 shows our suggestion, where we are using thermocol (1.5"), plywood (6mm), J-hooks, washers and bolts. The bottom of the bolts should be covered with caps to give aesthetic view. This is a durable solution as compared to the thermocol placed over the roof.
- Height of the topmost slab should be at least 3.10m

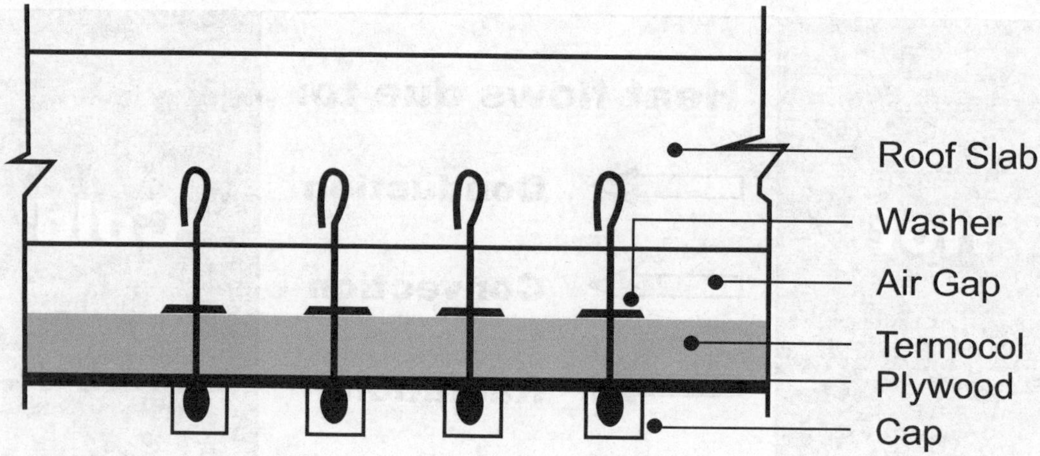

Fig.6.3: Insulation for roof

6.3.4. Selection of site

The project set up is done a selected room of ceramic centre of Bikaner.

Fig.6.4: Site of project work

Dimension of room:-

a. Room Length- 19ft.

b. Room width - 14ft.

c. Room Height –12ft.

d. Window dimension 4x10(right)

e. Window dimension 4x6(left)

Fig.6.5: Inside view of site room

Fig.6.6: Water beg on roof of site

6.3.5 Setup procedure

a. Note down the temperature of the room in normal condition without any insulation for one week.

b. Note down the temperature when the room provide insulation with water begs on the roof for next one week

c. Note down continues reading per hour interval.

d. Compare the readings plotting curve between normal and insulated condition.

6.3.5.1 Temperature Reading (May 2010)

(a) Readings at normal condition:

Day-1

Time (a.m.-p.m.)	Face1	Face2	Face3	Face4	Room	Atm.	Outside wall
8-9	31.2	30.8	30.9	31.0	32.1	32.5	33.8
1-2	34.1	33.9	34.2	33.7	33.9	40.8	41.9
6-7	34.6	35.0	34.8	35.2	34.1	36.2	36.9

Day-2

Time (a.m.-p.m.)	Face1	Face2	Face3	Face4	Room	Atm.	Outside wall
8-9	30.2	30.8	31.0	30.8	31.2	31.5	33.3
1-2	34.3	34.2	34.1	34.2	34.2	39.8	40.2
6-7	34.8	35.2	34.9	36.5	34.7	38.7	38.9

Day-3

Time (a.m.-p.m.)	Face1	Face2	Face3	Face4	Room	Atm.	Outside wall
8-9	31.1	30.9	30.8	31.0	30.8	32.2	33.8
1-2	33.9	33.7	34.0	33.7	33.8	40.2	41.5
6-7	34.4	34.6	35.0	35.8	35.1	36.2	36.8

Day-4

Time (a.m.-p.m.)	Face1	Face2	Face3	Face4	Room	Atm.	Outside wall
8-9	31.3	31.4	31.0	31.2	31.9	32.2	33.6
1-2	35.1	35.3	35.0	35.4	35.6	41.9	42.5
6-7	34.8	35.2	34.8	35.7	35.1	37.9	37.0

Day-5

Time (a.m.-p.m.)	Face1	Face2	Face3	Face4	Room	Atm.	Outside wall
8-9	32.0	31.9	32.2	32.1	33.8	34.1	35.0
1-2	37.8	38.1	38.2	37.9	38.3	46.1	47.0
6-7	36.8	36.5	36.4	36.6	36.3	38.9	39.1

Day-6

Time (a.m.-p.m.)	Face1	Face2	Face3	Face4	Room	Atm.	Outside wall
8-9	31.7	32.1	32.0	31.8	32.2	34.2	35.3
1-2	37.9	38.0	38.3	38.1	38.4	46.3	47.2
6-7	36.9	36.7	36.6	37.1	36.4	39.0	39.3

Day-7

Time (a.m.-p.m.)	Face1	Face2	Face3	Face4	Room	Atm.	Outside wall
8-9	31.9	32.0	31.8	32.0	33.2	34.1	35.3
1-2	38.0	38.1	37.9	38.3	38.6	46.7	47.1
6-7	36.7	36.9	36.8	37.0	36.6	39.1	39.4

(b) Readings with waters begs:

Day-1

Time (a.m.-p.m.)	Face1	Face2	Face3	Face4	Room	Atm.	Outside wall
8-9	32.8	33.1	32.7	32.9	33.1	35.9	34.7
1-2	36.4	36.1	36.2	36.4	36.2	42.8	43.2
6-7	35.8	35.9	36.0	36.1	35.9	38.2	38.9

Day-2

Time (a.m.-p.m.)	Face1	Face2	Face3	Face4	Room	Atm.	Outside wall
8-9	31.3	31.4	31.0	31.2	31.9	32.2	33.6
1-2	35.1	35.3	35.0	35.4	35.6	41.9	42.6
6-7	34.8	35.2	34.8	35.7	35.1	37.9	38.2

Day-3

Time (a.m.-p.m.)	Face1	Face2	Face3	Face4	Room	Atm.	Outside wall
8-9	31.1	30.9	30.8	31.0	30.8	32.2	33.8
1-2	35.1	35.1	35.3	35.2	35.2	42.2	42.9
6-7	34.3	34.2	34.1	34.3	34.1	37.2	37.8

Day-4

Time (a.m.-p.m.)	Face1	Face2	Face3	Face4	Room	Atm.	Outside wall
8-9	32.6	33.2	32.8	32.7	32.3	35.8	34.3
1-2	36.2	36.3	36.5	36.7	36.6	42.8	43.1
6-7	36.5	36.3	35.9	36.0	36.3	39.2	40.6

Day-5

Time (a.m.-p.m.)	Face1	Face2	Face3	Face4	Room	Atm.	Outside wall
8-9	34.8	34.9	34.7	34.8	34.9	36.3	36.3
1-2	36.3	36.2	36.2	36.1	36.3	42.6	43.7
6-7	36.1	36.1	36.0	36.2	36.1	40.2	41.3

Day-6

Time (a.m.-p.m.)	Face1	Face2	Face3	Face4	Room	Atm.	Outside wall
8-9	31.2	30.8	30.9	31.0	32.1	32.5	33.8
1-2	34.1	33.9	34.2	33.7	33.9	39.8	40.1
6-7	34.6	35.0	34.8	35.1	34.5	36.2	37.1

Day-7

Time (a.m.-p.m.)	Face1	Face2	Face3	Face4	Room	Atm.	Outside wall
8-9	34.6	34.5	34.5	34.7	34.6	36.3	35.8
1-2	35.9	36.3	35.8	36.0	36.6	39.1	41.4
6-7	36.2	36.1	36.2	36.0	36.2	37.4	39.9

(c) Continuous per hour's readings

Temperature measurement without water begs

Day 1

Time (a.m.-p.m.)	Face1	Face2	Face3	Face4	Room	Atm.	Outside wall
6:00	28.0	28.1	28.0	28.2	28.1	27.6	27.3
7:00	29.1	29.3	29.2	29.2	29.1	28.0	27.8
8:00	30.2	30.1	30.1	30.0	30.2	28.9	28.2
9:00	33.3	33.4	33.2	33.1	32.9	34.6	33.9
10:00	34.6	34.5	34.5	34.7	34.6	36.3	35.8
11:00	36.5	36.4	36.7	36.6	36.5	36.8	38.3
12:00	36.6	36.5	36.5	36.4	37.2	38.3	39.9
1:00	36.9	36.8	36.8	37.0	37.3	38.7	39.3
2:00	36.9	36.7	37.2	36.9	37.4	39.1	41.4
3:00	37.1	36.8	36.6	36.7	36.8	38.9	41.7

4:00	37.5	37.5	37.6	37.4	37.5	41.3	43.4
5:00	37.6	37.4	37.5	37.6	37.2	40.9	42.5
6:00	36.9	36.8	36.8	36.7	36.9	38.9	40.6
7:00	36.5	36.4	36.3	36.5	36.4	37.4	39.7
8:00	35.8	35.8	35.7	35.9	35.9	34.7	37.0
9:00	34.9	34.8	34.9	34.8	34.9	34.2	34.9
10:00	33.5	33.4	33.5	33.6	33.3	32.9	33.2

Temperature measurement with water begs

Day 1

Time (a.m.-p.m.)	Face1	Face2	Face3	Face4	Room	Atm.	Outside wall
6:00	27.1	27.0	27.2	27.0	27.0	27.6	27.3
7:00	28.2	28.1	28.1	28.0	28.2	28.0	27.8
8:00	29.8	29.8	29.7	29.9	29.1	28.9	28.2
9:00	31.2	31.1	31.2	31.2	31.2	34.6	33.9
10:00	32.7	32.8	32.9	32.8	33.2	36.3	35.8
11:00	35.5	35.3	35.4	35.3	35.4	36.8	38.3
12:00	36.0	36.1	36.2	36.1	36.0	38.3	39.0
1:00	36.2	36.3	36.5	36.4	36.2	38.7	39.6
2:00	36.4	36.5	36.7	36.4	36.5	39.1	41.4
3:00	35.7	35.9	35.8	35.8	35.6	38.9	41.7
4:00	36.8	36.9	36.8	37.0	36.8	41.3	43.4
5:00	36.5	36.2	36.2	36.1	36.1	40.9	42.5
6:00	35.8	35.7	35.9	35.6	35.7	38.9	40.6
7:00	35.0	35.1	35.1	35.0	35.0	37.4	39.7
8:00	34.8	34.7	34.9	34.6	34.7	34.7	37.0
9:00	33.9	33.8	33.7	33.9	34.0	34.2	34.9
10:00	32.5	32.3	32.1	32.0	32.1	32.9	33.2

Temperature measurement with water begs

Day 2

Time (a.m.-p.m.)	Face1	Face2	Face3	Face4	Room	Atm.	Outside wall
6:00	29.4	29.5	29.4	29.6	29.5	29.1	28.6
7:00	30.7	30.8	30.8	30.9	30.8	30.5	29.9
8:00	32.1	32.2	32.2	32.1	32.1	32.8	33.0
9:00	34.8	34.9	34.7	34.8	34.5	36.3	36.3
10:00	35.4	35.3	35.2	35.2	35.3	39.4	37.1
11:00	36.0	35.8	35.8	35.9	35.9	39.4	39.8
12:00	36.1	36.0	35.9	36.0	36.0	39.8	41.2
1:00	36.3	36.2	36.2	36.1	36.3	42.6	43.7
2:00	36.2	36.3	36.2	36.4	36.4	43.2	44.5
3:00	36.3	36.4	36.4	36.2	36.6	43.9	45.0
4:00	36.2	36.2	36.1	36.3	36.3	43.7	44.7
5:00	36.1	36.2	36.1	36.2	36.1	42.9	43.8
6:00	35.8	35.9	35.7	35.8	35.8	42.2	43.3
7:00	35.1	35.2	35.2	35.3	35.1	40.3	41.0
8:00	34.8	34.9	34.8	34.7	34.8	38.2	40.1
9:00	33.8	33.8	33.7	33.9	33.9	36.4	37.3
10:00	32.7	32.8	32.8	32.9	32.7	34.8	36.0

Temperature measurement without water begs

Day 2

Time (a.m.-p.m.)	Face1	Face2	Face3	Face4	Room	Atm.	Outside wall
6:00	30.5	30.4	30.4	30.6	30.5	29.1	28.6
7:00	32.3	32.1	32.0	32.3	32.3	30.5	29.9
8:00	32.7	32.8	32.7	32.9	33.1	32.8	33.0
9:00	35.6	35.8	35.7	35.6	35.6	36.3	36.3

10:00	36.8	36.7	36.9	37.0	36.9	39.4	37.1
11:00	36.9	37.0	37.1	36.9	37.0	39.4	39.8
12:00	36.8	36.9	37.1	37.0	37.1	39.8	41.2
1:00	37.2	37.3	37.4	37.3	37.4	42.6	43.7
2:00	37.7	37.6	37.4	37.6	37.6	43.2	44.5
3:00	37.4	37.6	37.5	37.4	37.5	43.9	45.0
4:00	37.1	37.2	37.0	37.1	37.2	43.7	44.7
5:00	36.9	36.8	37.0	37.1	37.0	42.9	43.8
6:00	37.0	36.9	37.0	36.8	36.7	42.2	43.3
7:00	36.4	36.5	36.4	36.3	36.4	40.3	41.0
8:00	335.9	35.8	35.8	35.9	35.9	38.2	40.1
9:00	35.0	35.1	35.2	35.0	35.0	36.4	37.3
10:00	33.8	33.9	33.7	33.9	33.9	34.8	36.0

6.3.5.2 Result & Discussion

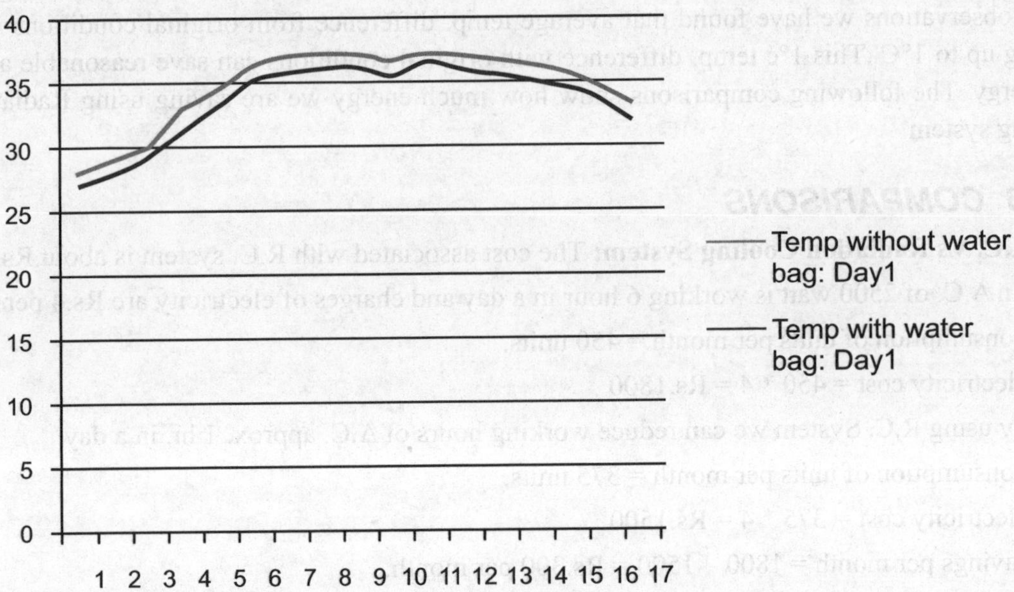

Fig.6.7: Temp. Vs. Time Curve (for inside room temp day 1)

(a) Without water begs

(b) With water begs

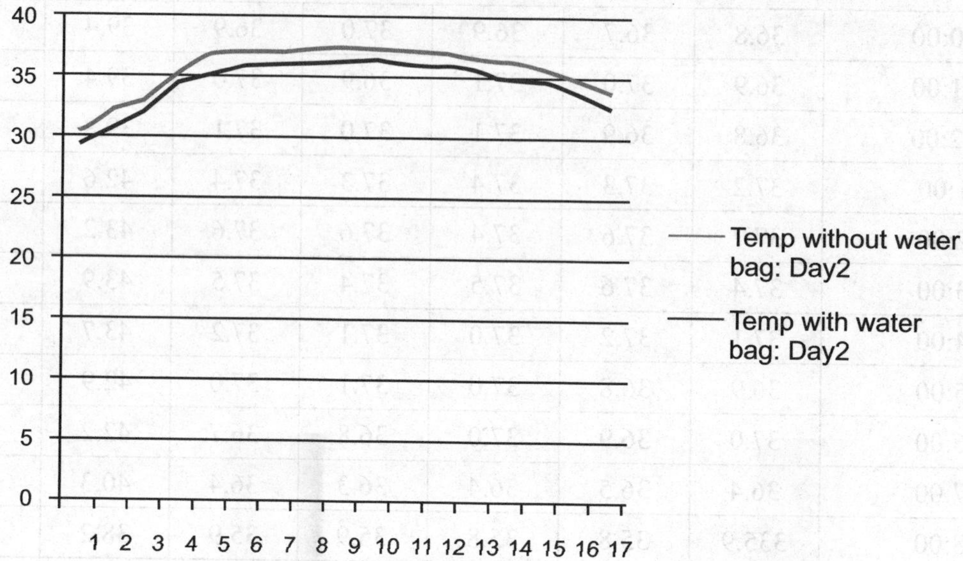

Fig.6.8: Temp. Vs. Time Curve (for inside room temp day 2)

(a) Without water begs

(b) With water begs

From observations we have found that average temp. difference from original conditions we are getting up to 1°C .This 1°c temp. difference with original conditions can save reasonable amount of energy. The following comparisons show how much energy we are saving using Radiation & cooling system.

6.3.6 COMPARISONS

1. **A.C. Vs Radiation Cooling System:** The cost associated with R.C. system is about Rs.1500

   An A.C. of 2500 watt is working 6 hour in a day and charges of electricity are Rs.4 per unit.

   Consumption of units per month = 450 units.

   Electricity cost = 450 * 4 = Rs.1800

   By using R.C. System we can reduce working hours of A.C. approx. 1 hr. in a day.

   Consumption of units per month = 375 units.

   Electricity cost = 375 * 4 = Rs.1500

   Savings per month = 1800 – 1500 = Rs.300 per month.

   Savings per year = 300 * 5 = Rs.1500 (Since we are using A.C. for 5 months.)

   If a building is having 10 living rooms , then by using this system annual saving will be = 1500 * 10 = Rs.15000

   Therefore, total saving will be = 15000 – 1500 = Rs.13500

2. **Cooler Vs. R.C System:** - A Cooler of 180 watt is working 10 hour in a day.

   Consumption of units per month = 54 units.

   Electricity cost = 54 * 4 = Rs.216

   By using R.C. System we can reduce working hours of Cooler approx. 2 hr. in a day.

   Consumption of units per month = 43.2 units.

   Electricity cost = 43.2 * 4 = Rs.172.8

   Savings per month = 216 – 172.8 = Rs.43.2 per month.

   Savings per year = 43.2 * 5 = Rs.216 (since we are using Cooler for 5 months)

   If a building is having 10 living rooms , then by using this system annual saving will be = 216 * 10 = Rs.2160

   Therefore, total saving will be = 2160 – 1500 = Rs.660

"***Thus from above comparison we conclude that radiation cooling system is much cheaper and energy saving than any other cooling system.***"

6.3.7 Discussion

1. It provides better quality of life to citizens even with the shortage of the energy.
2. Effort will be made to refine existing sites for simulated results and eco-friendly performance.
3. The temperature variation in building due to global warming can be reduced.
4. It is seen that evaporative cooling on the roof leads to a net saving in the initial investment and in the annual cost.
5. It can be easily used in exiting building with minimum cost in summer.

6.3.8 Recommendations and Scope for Future Work

- Micro studies regarding the Radiation energy liberated by various appliances and including it in analysis.
- Insulating the entire room with a suitable insulating material and then calculating the heat infiltration and finding its deviation from the current result obtained.
- Analyzing the current electrical devices and suggesting better cost saving devices and also looks into its controls and positions from ergonomic point of view.
- Coating the roof with proper insulating material to reduce incoming heat.
- Installing better heat resisting fiber or glass in doors and windows.

References

1. A. Adarve. E. Mayer and P. Rivet. (1987). Natural Ventilation in Equatorial Developing Countries. Proc. of ISES Solar World Congress, Hamburg, FRG.
2. A.A.M Singh (1979). "Solar Energy Application in Building." Academic Press, New York.
3. A.F.C. Sherratt (1969). "Air Conditioning System Design for Building". Elsevier Publishing Company Ltd. New York.
4. A.K. Gupta and Surbhi Gaur. (2003). "Energy Efficient Buildings". A Seminar Organized by JNVUL, Jodhpur,
5. A.K. Gupta, SaurabhVarshney. (2004). "Energy Efficiency in Low Cost Housing". Journal of IndianBuilding Congress, Vol. XI. No.1.
6. Aboulanga, M.M. and Abdrabboh, S.N. (2000)."Improving Night Ventilation into Low-rise Building in Hot-Arid Climates Exploring a Combined Wall-Solar Chimney". Renewable Energy, Vol. 19, Adnan.
7. Ahmad, Adil Mustafa. (1975). The Thermal Performance of Concrete Roofs and Reed Shading Panels Under Arid Summer Conditions. Overseas Building Notes. No. 164. BRS Watford, England.
8. ASHRAE Handbook (1981), Fundamentals.
9. B. Givoni, Man.(1976). Climate and Architecture. Applied Science Publishers Ltd., London.
10. Bahadori, M.N. (1978). Passive Cooling System in Iranian Architecture. Ibid.
11. Bakiwala, V. (2002). Case Studies of Earth Air Tunnels in India. B.Arch. Dissertation at Malaviya National Institute of Technology, Jaipur.
12. Bakos, G.C., Soursos, M. and Tsagas, N.F. (2003). "Technoeconomic assessment of a building integrated PV system for electrical energy saving in residential sector". Energy Build. 35 (8).
13. Balcomb, J.D. (1978). "Passive Solar Design Handbook". Report No. DOE/CS 0127/182.
14. Balcomb, J.D. and McFarland, R.D. (1978). "A Simple Empirical Method for Estimating the Performance of a Passive Solar Heated Building of a Thermal Storage Wall Type, Proc. 2nd National Passive Solar Conference.

15. Bansal, N.K. and Minke, G. (1988). "Climatic Zones and Rural Housing in India". Julich.
16. Bansal, N.K. and Minke, G. (1995). Climatic Zones and Rural Housing in India, Research Centre, Juelich, Germany.
17. Bansal, N.K., Hauser, G. and Minke, G. (1994). "PassiveBuilding Design". Elsevier Science, B.V.
18. Bhadadori, M.N. (1979). Natural Cooling in Hot Arid Regions. Solar Energy Applications in Building. AAM Sayigh, Editor. Academic Press, New York.
19. Bhardwaj, S.S. and Bansal, N.K. (1981). Temperature Distribution Inside Ground for Various Surface Conditions. Buildings and Environment, No. 610. Pergamon Press.
20. BLAST. (1977). Building Loads Analysis and System Thermodynamic Program. Vol. 1.
21. Bonneville Power Administration (1991). "Reducing Power Factor Cost." Technology Update.
22. Bonneville Power Administration (1993). "Energy Efficient Motor Selection." Handbook.
23. Bureau of Indian Standards, IS: 3362. (1965). Code of Practice for Natural Ventilation of Residential Buildings, New Delhi, India.
24. Bureau of Indian Standards. (1987). Handbook of Functional Requirements of Buildings. ISBN 81-7061-01-7, New Delhi, India.
25. C. Karakatsanis, M.N. Bhadori and B.J. Vickery. (1986). Evaluation of Pressure Coefficients and Estimation of Air Flow Rate in Buildings Employing wind towers. Solar Energy, Vol. 37 No. 5.
26. C. Mc. Crave & S.D. Probert. (1996). "Some Economically Viable Techniques for the Reduction of Energy Expenditure in British Public Houses", Applied Energy, Vol. 554, No. 1. Elsvier Science Ltd. Great Britain.
27. C.E.A. Winslow. (1926). Objective and Standards of Ventilation. ASHVE Journal, Vol. 32.
28. C.Mc. Crave & S.D. Probert. (1996). "Some Economical Viable Techniques for Reduction of Energy Expenditure in British Public Houses." Applied Energy. Vol. 54, Elsevier Science Ltd. Great Britain.
29. C.P. Yaglou and W.N. Witheridge. (1936). Ventilation Requirements. ASHVE Trans., Vol. 43.
30. C.P. Yaglou. (1955). ASHRAE Trans. 42.
31. Carslaw, H.C. and Jaegor, J.C. (1959). "Conduction of Heat in Solids". OxfordUniversity Press.
32. CASAMO. (1982). User's Manual, Ecole de Mines de Paris, Armines, Paris.
33. CEN. (1991). Residential Buildings Energy Requirements for Heating Calculation Method, CEN TC 89-WG4 N61, European Prestandard.
34. CII-GBC. (2004). Pocket Guide on Green Buildings. CII- Sohrabji Godrej Business Centre, Hyderabad, India.
35. Clarke, J.A. and Maver T.W. (1991). Advanced Design Tools for Energy Conscious Buildings Design: Development and Dissemination, Building and Environment. 26(1).

36. Cross, N. (1986). Understanding Design: The Lesson of Design Methodology, Design Methods and Theories.

37. D.J. Croome and B.M. Roberts. (1981). Air-Conditioning and Ventilation of Buildings. Pergamon Press.

38. DajithaSimha (1985). "Building Environment" Tata Mchraw Hill Publishing Company Ltd., New Delhi.

39. Danter, E. (1960). "Periodic Heat Flow Characteristics of Simple Walls & Roofs" J. IHVE, Vol. 28.

40. David Wright. (1978). Natural Solar Architecture- A passive primer. Litton Educational Publishing New York.

41. DebajitPalit. (2004). GreenBuilding. The Assam Tribune.

42. Donald R., Wulfinghoff, P.E. (2002). How to Build & Operate a Super Efficient House. Wulfinghoff Energy Services. Inc., Maryland.

ENERGY CONSERVATION IN BUILDINGS

O.P. JAKHAR

FEEDBACK FORM

1. Which topics from your examination point of view are inadequately or not covered in this book?

____

____

2. Is there any misprints/ mistakes/ factual inaccuracy in this book? If so, please specify.

____

____

3. What is your assessment of this book as regards the presentation of the subject-matter, expression, precision and price in relation to the other recommended books available on this subject?

____

____

4. Which competing books you regard as better than this? Please mention their author and publishers.

____

____

5. Any further suggestions/comments you would like to make for the improvement of the book?

____

____

***PS:** If needed, please attach a separate sheet.*

Name : ____________________

College : ____________________

Address : ____________________

Email : ____________________

Mobile : ____________________

Please mail the feedback form at:

KHANNA BOOK PUBLISHING CO. (P) LTD.

4C/4344, Ansari Road, Daryaganj, New Delhi-110002

You can also email this feedback form at contact@khannabooks.com or Whatsapp at +91 – 99109 09320

BEST FEEDBACK WILL BE REWARDED SUITABLY